THE
CORPORATE
SHAMAN

THE CORPORATE SHAMAN

A Business Fable

Richard Whiteley

HarperBusiness
An Imprint of HarperCollins*Publishers*

HarperCollins books may be purchased for educational, business, or sales promotional use. For information please write: Special Markets Department, HarperCollins Publishers, Inc., 10 East 53rd Street, New York, NY 10022.

FIRST EDITION

Designed by Nancy Singer Olaguera

Library of Congress Cataloging-in-Publication Data has been requested.

ISBN   0-06-000839-3

02 03 04 05 06 QW/❖ 10 9 8 7 6 5 4 3 2 1

To all shamans everywhere who, throughout the ages, have
lovingly created healing in those they serve.

This book could not have been written without the wisdom and guidance of many teachers. I extend deep thanks and appreciation to Edward Agpaoa, Geo Cameron, David Corbin, Tom Cowan, Michael Harner, Sandra Ingerman, Ipu, Serge Kahili King, Jun Labo, Jaime Licauco, Lewis Mehl-Madrona, Nan Moss, and John Perkins.

I honor my spirit teachers and power animals for the insights and guidance they have provided at critical crossroads in the creation of *The Corporate Shaman.*

Shayla Roberts, a powerful healer in her own right, put words to paper to bring *The Corporate Shaman* to life. Shayla rendered the story, characters, and concepts in simple and imaginative prose, enriching the original storyboard from her own store of wisdom gained over the years as a personal counselor and executive coach.

Also Janet Berrien, Ken Blanchard, Marge Blanchard, Bob Bohem, John Bray, Joanne Brem, Stephen Bonner, Peter Hillyer, Lee Hubbard, John Humphrey, Christie Jacobs, David Kulow, Patricia McLagan, Marcia Radosevich, Ann Rice, Patricia Pomerleau, and Sharon Whiteley.

Joe Veltre of HarperCollins brought both an open mind

and editorial wisdom to the project. His thoughts, suggestions, and willingness to adapt were most helpful.

Betsy Lerner is a wonderful agent and person. She not only represented the book, but her keen insights helped shape the final product.

It is with pleasure and gratitude that a portion of the proceeds from *The Corporate Shaman* will be donated to the Foundation for Shamanic Studies, a non-profit organization dedicated to bringing the healing practices of shamanism to people around the world.

CONTENTS

Welcome

1

Addendum

131

WELCOME

"Shaman" (pronounced SHAH-mahn) is a word of the Tungis people of Siberia which means "one who sees in the dark." Shamans are healers, and there is archaeological evidence of their work as far back as forty thousand years ago. Often known by other names, including, "witch doctor," "sorcerer," "wizard," "medicine man," and "kahuna kapua," these people can be found practicing their healing methods throughout the entire world. In virtually every culture, from England to Korea and from Iceland to Brazil, you will find these remarkable practitioners plying their trade.

A shaman is one who enters an altered state of mind, at will, and journeys to other worlds and uses the power, wisdom, and energies of those other worlds to create positive change in people and the environments in which they live. Their work is empirical in that it is based on trial and error over tens of thousands of years. With the wisdom and efficacy of such work being continually distilled and improved and then handed down through the generations, we have available to us today very powerful, proven processes that can be used for divination (finding the solutions to problems) or healing.

As allies in their healing work, shamans rely on teachers and power animals from the realms to which they journey. The journey is a meditative process by which the shaman gains access to these other worlds. By connecting with these compassionate and healing spirits the shaman becomes the conduit or "hollow bone" through which the healing energies and messages are transmitted.

The story of PRIMETEC, Inc., is a composite of real people in real situations. The pressures and resulting anxiety felt by the people in this high-tech company are typical of the tensions experienced by many people in many companies around the world today.

Since shamanic practices are aimed at healing individuals and since organizations like PRIMETEC are nothing more than groups of individuals, it follows that these powerful methods can be used to heal and restore spirit to organizations, which is, indeed, happening. All the shamanic practices described in the pages that follow are real and have been refined over many millennia. A number of them have already been adapted for use in helping organizations achieve their true potential.

ONE

A sacred pathway of drumbeats opens into three worlds where spirit shows itself in many forms and opens minds. A drummer holds the pathway steady, as Shaman slips into the middle world. This place is a portal—a depot where journeys to the upper and lower worlds begin. Yet, sometimes suffering souls abide here dead or alive, isolated from their sources of health and power. Shaman enters undaunted, tethered to safety by the drum path he walks and steeped in the wisdom he has learned from the ages.

He comes upon a man who is choking, his own hands crushing his neck, thumbs pressing to throat as though to force some painful truth to the surface. Shaman asks, "Why are you strangling yourself?" The throttled head does not hear, does not answer.

Leon King, the CEO of PRIMETEC, Inc., pointedly surveyed the faces that circled the boardroom table that August morning. He was in no mood for niceties, but to his credit he did say, "Well, good morning, people." The slight lift resulting from this acknowledgement was quashed seconds later when he continued sternly, "I'm going to cut to the chase." He paused with a studied stare in the direction of Mark Steed, his vice president of operations. There was a detail he needed to address. "Mark has asked me to say some nice words about Marion Crowley and what she's accomplished in her department. Normally, I would be happy to do that, but it's not appropriate to this morning's agenda. The time to throw bouquets is after we make the numbers, not before." He stopped and said with grave emphasis, "And people, we're not making the numbers.

"This morning we're going over this one more time so we're all on the same page with what's happening here," he said, glancing almost imperceptibly at a notepad he had carried in with him. He began reciting the facts. "We're in a strong economy, with industry growth at sixteen percent. PRIMETEC's growth is at seven percent. Our costs are rising faster than revenues. We laid off three hundred people just six months ago and it looks like we may need to downsize again. Turnover in the industry is sixteen percent. We're at twenty-nine."

He picked up a quarterly report from the table and waved it in the air. "Our margins are shrinking and our last new product is underperforming against pro forma sales figures. We've been riding on the success of our initial products, but this cash cow is running out of milk and we've been unable to come up with new product successes. And it doesn't help that we've lost some key performers, particularly in the sales force."

His throat seemed to catch slightly. He cleared it and continued, "Short-term, we're going to miss our numbers this quarter . . . again! And our projections for the last quarter have us sixteen percent below target."

He tucked his chin slightly, lowering his brow so that his

eyes glowered from beneath, and placed the report back on the table in a slow, deliberate manner. His hand remained arched over the report cover like a spider, his index finger ominously tapping out a cadence that underscored what he said next: "This just isn't acceptable."

King's tone dramatized the degree to which he took the situation personally. The way he looked at it, the numbers were a direct reflection of his worth as a CEO. When PRIMETEC missed its numbers, he felt he might as well have a sign around his neck saying, "I'm incompetent." He tugged at his collar as though to adjust the condemning placard and paced several steps, his shoes making the only sound in the frozen silence.

"Yesterday I made a commitment to the analysts down on Wall Street. I assured them PRIMETEC will make its numbers. So now those numbers are much more than just a target. They're a promise—my promise. Do you hear me, people? I've written a check to Wall Street." His eyes targeted each person in the room. "And you are going to cash that check."

The day, like most, had started early for King, the sky still showing stars when he stepped out onto the balcony of his rambling Scarsdale, New York, home. He breathed in the cool air and gazed red-eyed across to the bedroom wing of the house, where his mind had been racing for hours in the dark. He had finally given in and gotten up.

He booted up his computer in the office behind him. It would be hours before NASDAQ opened, but even a game of digital solitaire was better than more of the emotional replays that had kept him awake for most of the night. Here, alone in the dark, he could admit it. He was scared. He felt he was holding the company together by sheer willpower. He'd walked into

Goldman Sachs as if into a casino and put PRIMETEC on the line. Now he'd have to do more than draw the right cards to make good on his bet. He would tighten the screws at every level of the organization: cut costs, hire and fire, retool if necessary, to turn things around and salvage his company—and his self-respect.

It was a miserable situation. The company's growth rate trailed that of the industry by nine percentage points. Costs were rising faster than revenues, and . . . no, he wouldn't go through the checklist again. The numbers stank, and he was sick of it. Better to save the grim details for the meeting. He clenched his teeth and went inside, closing the door behind him forcefully. He would let them have it, the whole executive team. They hadn't been there for him in months, and he was going to come down hard. If his temper ran the meeting, too bad! No more Mister Nice Guy.

"Nice guy" wasn't exactly what came to mind when John Conatello thought about Leon King these days. As VP of sales, John often had had to spar with Leon, and even more often since PRIMETEC lost its president, Mel Hawkins, six months back. John joked to friends that King was sharp as a tack and hard as nails. "With that at the top of the ladder," he'd say, "it's no wonder he's up there by himself."

John was a seasoned sales professional. He'd earned King's trust years ago when he first talked his way up from the showroom floor, but he no longer felt he was getting through to King. "If he'd just ease up a little," he said to his wife, Liz, as he folded the morning paper and pushed back from the table, "A little bad press when Hawkins resigned in February, and he's been clamping down ever since. He was down on Wall Street yesterday, so

I'm sure we're going to see fireworks this morning. And human resources still hasn't been able to replace Hansen and Clift for me. It won't be good going into that meeting empty-handed."

He disappeared down the hall and emerged moments later with briefcase in hand. "I'll try to make Kevin's game tonight," he said and left for work punching in Helen Singer's number on his cell phone. His wife knew that his making the game was worse than a long shot. John hadn't showed up at one all season.

Helen Singer had been in the building for over an hour. She was troubleshooting an insurance crisis that was impacting the whole organization. Vice president of human resources. How she had coveted the position, and what a headache it had become over the last year and a half! She finally got a moment to check her phone messages, and grimaced slightly when she heard: "Hi, Helen, John here, sorry I missed you. It's important that we talk before the meeting today. You can reach me on my cell phone."

He wants answers on our open-to-hires in sales, she thought to herself. Too early to reach anybody about the rep position in San Francisco. She looked at her watch to see if anyone would be around yet in Cleveland, then called for a status report on the district manager opening there. Nearly two months, still no luck, and sales were down. "Okay," she said, "let me know if anything changes," and hung up.

She sipped her third cup of coffee, noticing that her right hand shook a little from caffeine as she dialed John's number. "I wish I had something new for you," she said when he answered.

"Listen, I know you've got a full agenda in HR," he replied, "but you know we're going to get pressure from Leon today. I was hoping to announce the new hires in the meeting."

Helen had the headhunting firm of Hemmings & Young beating the bushes, but the market was strong and competition for good people was fierce. "Sorry," she said. "With a strong economy, good people are just hard to find."

John sighed his disappointment.

Helen wasn't looking forward to the meeting either. "I hope Leon isn't thinking about another layoff," she said, revealing her own concern. "Morale is low enough already."

Helen had been King's closest confidante at PRIMETEC for over five years. When they first met, he'd found her easy to talk to, and soon he was seeking her out whenever he needed a friendly ear. In recent months, though, he had distanced himself. At about the same time, he had started chopping heads as a way of cutting costs while Helen believed PRIMETEC was getting too thin. She didn't enjoy wielding a hatchet, but she could perform the task with precision when it was necessary. She simply hadn't been able to justify most of the recent layoffs in her own mind, and with little access to King, her views had gone unexpressed. She wasn't sure how she'd react if he ordered another downsizing. It made her restless to think about it.

She was also concerned about the man himself. She saw him getting more and more stressed. He'd adopted a defensive, bullying posture that seemed out of character and was alienating people just when he needed their support.

Helen was a natural leader in her own right who valued the people on her team. As a result, HR operated like a well-oiled machine with strong morale and good support to the rest of the organization.

"Look," she said, finishing up with John, "I'll try to reach someone in San Francisco before the meeting. Maybe they've got some good news."

She clicked off her headset and opened her e-mail to see if there were any new messages from the West Coast. Her eyes softened into a smile when she came across a familiar communiqué from Maria Martinez. It was a little e-mail drawing made up of symbols and letters, a signal Maria had devised to let Helen know she wanted a huddle before an impending audience with "the King," as she had come to call him lately. So, thought Helen, Maria's nervous about this one too. I wonder what's up in marketing.

Helen and Maria both knew the drill: a ten-minute walk to clear their minds and sharpen their wits right before the meeting. They had developed an open, candid friendship over the years, trusting each other with confidences most people in their positions would have saved for friends outside of work. They had risen up the corporate ladder together and were able executives who could bang heads with the best of them when necessary, but they found their brief walks helpful. It seemed that King was growing more intense at every meeting and more likely to question everyone's performance. Helen hit "reply" and assured Maria she would be available.

The chief financial officer at PRIMETEC was preparing for the meeting in his own way. He scrutinized the quarterly report one more time, making sure he was clear on the rationale that substantiated one of the columns of numbers.

Frank Farratt was a small man with the pinched face of a Doberman, and, indeed, he was the watchdog at PRIMETEC. He had come on board as CFO shortly after Leon founded the company. They had known each other in college, and they still played the roles they had assumed there. Leon was always out front, the winning athlete, popular with the women. Frank, studious but socially awkward, had latched onto Leon in their sophomore year, hoping to make himself useful so he could be part of the flurry of activity that always surrounded King. Frank soon discovered King's fascination with business and came forward with his own expertise in finance. He crunched his first serious numbers in support of a video rental operation King ran on campus. To this day, Frank ran interference for King and could be counted on to back every decision Leon made with calculated facts and numbers. There had been a time about a year ago when Frank saw King getting soft on the numbers, but he'd found a way to wake him up and was certain that things were getting back on track.

Helen held the heavy glass entrance door open and pointed knowingly back at Maria, who was just a step behind. Helen was indicating in a playful way that since Maria had called for this little walk it was she who should start the conversation. As they fell into a brisk stride down the sidewalk, Maria laughed and said, "Okay, here's what's going on."

Maria was PRIMETEC's vice president of marketing. She was a small woman with an outrageous mop of red hair. She was a fireball, the life of every party, and on the job she was a power to reckon with. Early in her career, she had shown an uncanny ability to penetrate the glass ceiling wherever she went, both in academia and in business. She was very smart and wise beyond her years, but the real keys to her success were her tireless energy and contagious enthusiasm. In recent weeks, however, she had seemed almost listless. Helen had been concerned and wasn't at all surprised when Maria's laugh faded and she turned somber. "I don't even know how to say this. I feel silly, as if I were making this up." Her huge dark eyes focused on her friend's face. "You'd tell me if I was getting the ax, wouldn't you?"

"What? Why on earth are you thinking that?" Helen replied.

"So I'm not?"

"Maria, there isn't one shred of evidence to point to the possibility that you're getting fired. Why are you worried about that all of a sudden?"

"It's really not all of a sudden," Maria said. "It's been keeping me up at night for weeks." Maria was concerned about how she would make it through the end of the year. As head of marketing, she was right in the middle of the numbers crisis. Her department was behind on all its deadlines in support of sales efforts. Her key people were nervous, looking to her for support, and she was exhausted.

"Well, let me put your mind at ease about one thing. You're not getting fired," said Helen. At least not as far as I know, she thought to herself, painfully aware that she didn't really know what King might be planning. When they came to the corner, a taxi swerved close to the curb and Helen instinctively stepped out in front of Maria as though to protect her. She knew Maria wasn't alone in her concerns. She was seeing it everywhere in PRIMETEC. People were afraid. There was too much pressure being applied from the top and not enough guidance.

Traffic cleared, and they quickly crossed the street against the light. "This is between you and me," Helen continued. "There have been many times when I haven't agreed with the way Leon runs things. But I think his actions lately are particularly questionable. He's got everybody worried about their jobs, and, truth is, if we started firing everyone who's not performing up to par right now, we'd have to build the company from scratch again."

"Well, I know for me it's immobilizing," said Maria. "It's

not what he wants that's unreasonable. It's how he asks for it. Sometimes he makes me feel like I'm about six years old, getting scolded by my father. It's the first time in my career that I'm not sure what to do."

"Whoa, don't I know! It's affecting everyone," said Helen, glancing at her watch. They started back, maintaining their quick pace. "I just get mad," Helen continued. "It takes everything I have sometimes to contain myself. And afterward, I'm no good for hours. Seriously, sometimes I think I would have been happier if I hadn't broken through the glass ceiling. Just when you think you know what's going on, everything changes."

Maria assumed Helen was referring to the way her relationship with Leon had changed. She knew they had been close, and it pained her to see Helen affected by Leon's new posture of indifference. She let the subject drop, though, and said, "Hey, listen, I really appreciate being able to ask you that question and get a straight answer. Thanks."

They made their way back to the building, and their conversation lightened as they compared notes on the miracles they were each expected to perform as leaders in the company. Helen teased about needing to learn magic tricks, and Maria said, "No kidding. You know what I've been doing?" She caught herself midsentence and covered her lips with her fingertips.

"What?" asked Helen.

"Oh . . . I never can keep my mouth shut."

"What? Tell me."

"Well," Maria answered cautiously, "I've been working with a . . . a kind of coach, I guess. I can't give you the details yet, but talk about magic! . . . I shouldn't say that—it's actually just common sense. Anyway, he's really helped me keep from going crazy lately."

She tried changing the subject, but Helen interrupted, "Wait a minute! You're not going to drop that into the conversation at the last minute and not tell me more, are you? What kind of a coach?"

"Well, his name's Jason Hand," said Maria, pushing the elevator button for the twenty-eighth floor. "I brought him in to help iron out some differences between key people on my staff, but I must say he's been more of a help to me than anyone else."

"Is he an executive coach?" Helen asked.

"Well, I thought he was," Maria replied, " but it turns out he's a whole lot more. Actually he's a shaman."

"A shaman!" Helen said in surprise, "What's a sha—"

She was interrupted by the elevator door opening and revealing several PRIMETEC employees on their way from the basement cafeteria back to their offices. Helen and Maria stepped into the elevator and rode in silence. When they stepped out onto the twenty-eighth floor, Maria nodded to Helen and said, "Thanks again, Helen. I'm so relieved." Their talk had put them both in a positive frame of mind—which they knew would be tested soon enough.

TWO

Shaman bows his head and passes by the choking man. He will not be needed here until those pained hands loosen their hold, until the ears can listen and the mouth can speak its own deeper truths. He rides the drumbeat into the lower world. To Shaman's eyes, this country wears a cloak of green—wet, warm, and fresh. Down through the dense canopy, resins drip on waxy leaves, the sacred formulations of the mother's natural medicine cabinet. Here he greets Raven and rides on, seeking to retrieve a missing soul part for a woman of his tribe.

The executive conference room was dark, chairs pushed into the table, a sign that this would be the first meeting of the day. Mark Steed arrived early, as he often did, carrying a dog-eared work file. He would use the time before the meeting to collect his thoughts and review his notes.

As head of operations, Mark had been a key driver behind the company's highly successful first product introduction. With it, PRIMETEC established a strong customer base by being first to market, but in recent years sales had begun to dwindle. The newer products had been late to market and were not measuring up. Mark was feeling pressured. He took his job very seriously, and was deeply disturbed by his department's declining effectiveness. He knew his boss would be loaded for bear coming into the meeting today, and while he wasn't looking forward to the shots that would be fired in his direction, he would take them to heart.

Waiting for the others to arrive, he leafed through reports from his manufacturing plants. Charleston was clearing some issues, but Albuquerque was still hopelessly behind. This isn't fun, he thought, it isn't fun at all.

Frank Farratt came in moments later with a stack of folders. "Leon will be a bit delayed," he said, in his usual curt manner. He offered Mark no further greeting as he placed a copy of the quarterly report at each place around the large mahogany table.

It was still a few minutes before ten when the rest of the executive team arrived. Maria and Helen brought the warm air of the street in with them, and John was finishing up a call on his cell phone as he stepped into the room. Everyone was careful to be on time for Leon's meetings, even though the CEO himself was nearly always late. The wait time normally gave them a chance to compare notes and engage in lighthearted banter, but this morning as they assembled there was little interaction.

It was clear when King finally arrived that he was going to take no prisoners. He was dressed as always with great care, but there was a purple flush to his face, a reflection of the wine he had downed the night before, hoping it might help him sleep.

King's initial summary of the company's grim status was only the beginning of a very tense meeting. There was steel in his eyes as he scanned the room and continued, "It's no secret that we've got serious short-term problems. His eyes found his first target. "Isn't that so, John?"

Conatello hated more than anything to be singled out like that, and Leon knew it. So did everyone else in the room. They all understood King was putting them on notice that he wouldn't be pulling any punches.

King kept going. "And we have long-term problems too, don't we?" He didn't need to mention Mark's name; the pointed look in Mark's direction was enough. It raised a pall of consternation in the room that showed itself as a wave of red faces and tense body language. King took note, satisfied that he had their attention.

"People, you know about these problems," he said. "We've talked about these problems, over and over again. So I have to ask you: Am I or am I not paying you to make those problems go away?" His timing was impressive. No one moved. No one answered.

In the aftermath of King's heated first words, Helen was holding back a tirade of her own. How dare he, she thought indignantly, as if his own actions, his own approach to management, weren't part of the problem. She wanted to stand up and give King what for, tell him the truth about his own culpability, but she knew that even when she had been his closest confidante such action would have been professional suicide. Instead, she began to deepen her breathing as a way of calming herself down. Her pen went to the notepad in front of her. If she had to take this time away from her desk, she would make it count for something by making notes for an article she was writing on leadership for *Human Resource* magazine. King, she thought, was presenting a perfect negative example.

John, already unnerved, was waiting for the other shoe to

drop. He knew King wasn't through with him, but he also knew, from long experience with the man, that his approach would soon shift from tactics of shame to unabashed command and control. So he wasn't at all surprised by what King said next: "John, you're going to ramp it up—get your sales people out pounding the pavement. You've got exactly twelve weeks to turn things around."

John started to respond, but Leon cut him off. "I know you've lost some good people. . . . Get over it. No more excuses. Your sales pipeline is down and you're going to fill it up. Find your opportunities and get involved personally. From now on, when I call you at any time, day or night, and ask you for your top ten sales situations, you're going to tell me in detail—in detail—what's going on with those accounts."

He was steamrolling now, and he barely paused for a breath. He cautioned John not to try to pass the responsibility off to his account executives and field people. "I'm holding you personally accountable," he said. "You bring those accounts home. It will be on your head if this company doesn't make up that sixteen percent by the end of the year."

The force of King's words stunned John. Never, even in their most heated exchanges, had his boss assumed such an unrelenting posture. It was demeaning and it made John want to lash out with heated words of his own. They were piling up in his throat and he might have let them fly if Leon hadn't abruptly turned his attention to Mark and said sharply, "And you're going to do the long-term fix."

Because he was entirely outcome-oriented, King didn't fully comprehend the many subtle processes involved in design, manufacturing, and distribution. He relied heavily on Mark's expertise in those areas. Over the last year, he had pressed Mark to cut his costs to the bone, but King was frustrated by his own lack of control over product issues. He wanted to push Mark as he had pushed John, but he'd learned that a heavy hand was counterproductive in Mark's case. Still, he eased up only slightly as he said, "You've got to figure out why we can't get our products out on time. And you've got to find out what the customers want and create a product that delivers it. It's not rocket science, is it?"

Mark shook his head as if to answer, "Of course not." He was confident, even in the face of King's tirade. He wasn't going to defend the performance of his department. It didn't come close to meeting his own standards. He'd been in the trenches for months trying to turn things around, and he was certain he was on much firmer ground than Leon ever could be when it came to operations.

He saw that his job for the next few minutes would be to keep his cool and not let Leon's restatement of the obvious get to him. He listened as King disgorged a litany of criticisms and edicts, ending, "Those last designs looked okay, they just didn't get out of your shop once they went in. It's like the great black hole. Take a look and revamp. Do whatever you've got to do to get your cycle times under control.

"This is elementary." There was exasperation in King's voice. "We shouldn't even have to discuss these things to make the numbers. You've got to deliver what John sells. Tighten down your lead times and your turnaround times on deliveries. I don't know how you're going to do that, but figure it out. Keep the plants going twenty-four hours a day if you have to."

Mark made a conscious effort to stay in a listening mode, but his mind began to wander, reviewing his own assessment of the situation. He'd already extended plant hours, and it hadn't helped. He'd put a tight squeeze on every aspect of production and delivery, with no noticeable improvement. It's not how we're executing our plays, he thought to himself, it's the plays themselves. We've got to come up with a whole new game plan.

In another part of the building, Jason Hand was executing a plan of his own. He was putting the final touches on his temporary office at PRIMETEC. He was two weeks into his contract as an executive coach working closely with Maria in marketing. He'd been referred to her by a mutual associate who had intrigued Maria with his description of Jason's approach. She was impressed when she met him—enough to hire him and honor his request for a rather unusual workspace. Now, in a remote corner of the twenty-sixth floor, he was unpacking the special tools he used, storing some in elegant baskets and setting others artfully around the room. By afternoon, he would be ready to receive visitors.

Jason had not yet met Mark Steed, but he would have been most interested in Mark's insight about developing a new game plan for operations. Neither man could know in that moment that providence would create an opportunity for Jason to make several meaningful contributions to Mark's new game plan within a few short weeks.

Mark was looking at Leon, but he suddenly realized he hadn't heard a word he was saying for several minutes. He pulled his attention back just in time to hear: "With the pressure from Wall Street we can't project a flat year. We have to grow, people. We absolutely have to grow."

Mark looked around the room and realized he wasn't the only one whose mind had wandered. Frank still posed attentively, but the others made no attempt to cover the fact that their thoughts were drifting. John gazed out the window, relieved that the focus was off him for a bit. Helen was still making notes. King might have guessed she was recording his words, but he would have been chagrined to learn she would use them to illustrate a negative point in her article. Maria seemed withdrawn, holding the lapel of her jacket close to her as though to protect herself from the icy energy that continued to grip the room.

Normally, King would have picked up on the fact that he'd lost his audience, but now he was completely self-absorbed. On his way into work that morning he'd prepared a loaded speech for each member of his team, and he wasn't going to quit until those speeches were given. He was in his own world at war, shooting round after round. He swung around to Maria and fired, "You're part of this too, Maria."

She was caught off guard and the force of his words caused her stomach to tighten, but she held her ground as the barrage continued. "You missed the mark with the last introduction. The collaterals were late and the coordination between you and Mark wasn't tight enough. You put us in a position where people were ordering product we couldn't deliver. And that's the kiss of death on a new product introduction. You must do the data collection in the market to position the new product for success."

What's new, Maria thought, her stomach churning. She felt as if she'd lost control of her department and was about to lose her breakfast too. It was all she could do to control herself. She tried to replay Helen's assurances that her job was secure, but she was only slightly calmed and she couldn't breathe quite right until King shifted his sights once again.

"Helen, I want those key positions in sales filled. Now! Recruit some people who can hit the ground running. There's no time for a training ramp up, so get some veterans in here. John's fighting an uphill battle, and you're way behind in your recruiting targets." Helen looked him straight in the eye, thinking that a real leader can afford to assume his share of responsibility when things go wrong.

Then, abruptly, King stopped as though to reload. He took a drink of water, visibly collecting his thoughts, and said, "It just seems this company has about a three-month slippage on everything that's supposed to be happening, and Frank here tells me that even the receivables are stretched out by over ninety days."

His eyes connected with Frank's in a way that suggested an understanding between them. He turned back to Conatello: "John, get your sales people to do double-time. I not only want them selling, I want them following up with receivables so we don't run into a cash crunch at the end of the year. You've got to help Frank here bring receivables in line with our original targets."

Frank was visibly smug, gazing at John with his eyelids at half-mast. There was always a certain amount of tension between the two of them, simply because of their very different styles, but the heat was being turned up and everyone in the room knew it. They were all hoping this meeting was about over.

King opened the report he had set on the table, leafed through a page or two, and looked up. "Well, the bottom line here," he said, "is that this will be a short meeting. The numbers are the numbers and there's not too much more to say. We're at risk here. If we don't turn things around, we lose credibility big-time on Wall Street. Our investors and our shareholders will lose faith. I don't have to tell you people we just can't afford to let that happen.

"I don't have the answers here. You have the answers—that's why I hired you. Go back and figure these things out. I want to hear from each of you every week. . . . That's right, every week. I want to know what your plan is and how you're executing that plan. John, as I told you, address those key accounts. Mark, tighten up your product introduction. Maria, you're going to report to me on marketing plans for the new product rollout. Helen, I want to hear sometime next week that John has the people he needs." Then in an effort to appear unbiased, he turned to Frank and said, "Frank, put your thumb down on the receivables. We're finished with being sloppy here."

You could almost hear the clink of empty ammunition shells on the floor as King stepped forward once more to close the report. He wasn't very popular at the moment, but he felt justified. He paused to survey the damage, then brought the meeting to a close. "I expect more from you people than what you've been delivering. Unless you have any questions, this meeting's over."

After a moment of awkward silence, the members of the executive committee began sluggishly lifting themselves from their places. It was clear that this meeting would not be over for a very long time in their minds. It had stirred up a maelstrom of questions, but none of them would be asked of Leon King. Though he demanded weekly reports, he had positioned himself too far from the front lines. He would not be privy to comprehensive accounts of the action there. If PRIMETEC won this battle, it would be because Leon's commanders in the field took up their own banners in spite of him.

THREE

In the lower world, Shaman sees a young girl wandering beneath a spread of banyan trees. In somber reverie, she bends to pluck a ripened dandelion. Raising it high, she watches it light up with sun splash—the fuzz luminous like ocean spray at dawn. She lowers it to her mouth and with a sturdy breath, sends forth a company of tiny wind dancers.

With the voice in his mind Shaman asks, "Are you the soul part I'm looking for?" He sits down at a respectful distance and waits for her to answer him in her own time. Fly songs cut through the silence. Bird cheer echoes endlessly from tree to tree. The enchantment of the jungle loosens its hold on the maiden. She turns slowly to Shaman, still watching and waiting. "Yes," she says. "I am the one."

As they emerged from the boardroom, the PRIMETEC executive committee provided a stark contrast to a dandelion's fanciful flight. There was no grace, no lightness of being, no gentle drift in the same direction. Each disappeared in haste to a different part of the building.

Maria needed emotional triage, and she knew it. The purpose of the "coaching" program Jason had proposed was to strengthen her leadership skills, but it was taking her deep into herself, bringing up painful memories from the past. She knew she couldn't reorganize the marketing department effectively as long as she was one of the walking wounded. Getting the personal support she needed was a top priority for her own peace of mind as well as for the welfare of the company.

She stopped by her office to free up some time in the afternoon. "I'll review the new ad campaign tomorrow," she told Ben, her assistant. She would be stretching her time line again, but she wasn't in a state of mind to make decisions that would impact the new rollout. She wanted a clear head for that. Somehow, she thought, I know I'm on the verge of a breakthrough. Maybe this feeling of being attacked by King is a gift in disguise. She called for an appointment with Jason and was heartened when she learned he would be available at three.

Back at his computer, Mark was on task. He opened his calendar and designated Fridays as his times to check in with King—every week for the next three months. He had his assistant set up a meeting of his key people for early the following week. "It's important that all my direct reports be here," he said. "Bring everyone in from the field, no exceptions." Then he considered various presentation ideas, looking for a way to engage and energize his team. He imagined himself in a locker room at halftime reworking a game plan with his players. He didn't have a clue what the new plays should be, but it was helpful thinking of himself as the coach, and he trusted that somehow the right plan would come together.

In recent months, Mark had been visited by a different image of himself as the coach, one full of shadows . . . like a gray winter day, the sun setting too early in the drizzle and cold. He imagined himself walking alone, despondent. His head-coaching contract had been canceled and he was leaving the stadium for the last time—in disgrace. He had tried to hang on and pull off a winning season, but it was beyond him.

Mark resolved to never let that happen. He would resign if he thought his own performance was limiting the department, but he would never let it go to the point where he was fired. He had seriously questioned whether he was the right person to turn operations around, but had decided to stay at least for a while. He hated to quit while he was losing and he knew his resignation would throw PRIMETEC even further into chaos.

After the meeting this morning, though, there was a part of him that was tempted to reconsider. Mark was his own worst critic. He put more than enough pressure on himself. He didn't need the added weight of his boss breathing down his neck. His mind was a little splintered, but he mustered discipline and focused on the task at hand. He would do all he could to set the stage for his team to create a win.

No one in the sales area that morning failed to realize that John Conatello was very upset when he returned from the boardroom. His voice had a tendency to carry even when he was in an amiable mood. When he stormed in spewing thunder, it was obvious that things had not gone well.

He was ranting on the phone to Helen, "What does he want from me?" He had called to ask if she had anything new on the open-to-hires, but the tempest inside him was blowing and Helen was getting a torrent of grief. He was furious at Leon for calling him to task like a ten-year-old. How could he take on the added pressure of having to report in every week? It took hours to organize the kinds of reports King would want, and he'd been told not to delegate any of it. His own time would be pressed just to ramp up sales. He needed to be out in the field with customers. Now he had an extra load of administrative details, never his strong suit. "I feel like I've been drafted into a foreign legion," he said sarcastically, "a bunch of marching bean counters. . . . And dammit, Helen, where are my new hires?"

"Wait a minute," she said with considerable force of her own. "I'm not the enemy here, and I'm doing what I can." Helen was still sorting out her own reaction to the morning meeting, and while she identified with John's frustration, she wasn't about to be victimized by it.

"It's just that I hate having to work so closely with Frank," John said, backing down a little. "We've never been very compatible, and I get nervous when I think about being directly accountable to him on the receivables. He'll be picky about everything I do . . . and I'm not sure I trust the guy."

"It's true," said Helen, "you and Frank are like night and day, but I think he's basically harmless. The last thing we need is for you to go off on him! Take some time to let this thing settle. Maybe Hemmings & Young will find your new people in the next few days. I'll let you know the minute I hear."

Helen was relieved when she hung up the phone. She often played a peacemaking role at PRIMETEC and quite enjoyed it, but the meeting that morning had forced her to look at her own reactions. She was surprised by how defensive she had been toward Leon. She almost laughed when she thought about the notes she'd taken. Where did that come from? she thought. She wasn't particularly concerned about getting her job done; in many ways meeting John's staffing needs was business as usual for her. No . . . she had to admit she was deeply troubled by Leon's indifference toward her. He had been pulling away for months, and she'd been in denial about it.

She had trusted that she was more to King than just an employee. She was his friend. Over the years, he had called her often in the evenings and on weekends, asking for her input on a variety of things. Most of their conversations were business-related, but she had helped him through some tough personal challenges as well.

There had been periods when he disappeared for a while, but eventually he would show up unexpectedly at her office with a lunch invitation and they would pick up where they left off. Her relationship with Leon had been a source of pride to her. She loved the fact that he trusted her, and she had to admit it was an ego boost to have the confidence of a person of his status.

Helen believed King had what it took to become a truly great leader, one of the new school who leads by involvement and example rather than command and control. She had coached him, helping him trust more and loosen up. There had been a period of time when he seemed to be getting it. Then, when Mel Hawkins resigned as president of the company, the *Wall Street Journal* ran an article critical of PRIMETEC and Leon retreated, cordoning himself off as though he were under siege.

She had tried a number of times to get through to him, but increasingly King had others run interference. Helen didn't mind being put off by Leon's assistant, but it galled her one afternoon when Leon sent Frank to cover something he would always have handled himself in the past. Still, it wasn't until today that she had noticed how isolated she felt. She shook her head at the notepad on her desk, thinking to herself, I guess I was petty about it. No, I'm not going to get down on myself for reacting. This isn't what I would choose, but it's possible I'm the enemy now, and if I know what's good for me, I'll keep a sharp eye out. Oh, I'm just getting paranoid, she decided, and shook it off. She called Hemmings & Young for a status report. No change; the search was still on.

Frank Farratt stood mesmerized by a large anaconda. He had a fascination with snakes. While many people were petrified of them and identified them with the embodiment of evil in the Garden of Eden, Frank appreciated their quiet power and the respect people had for them. Although he would never consider keeping one as a pet, he had discovered a shop not far from the office that specialized in exotic species. He liked to go there when he needed time to think. No barking or chirping, just the silent motion of lithe forms doubling back on themselves.

The anaconda was a huge thing, over eight feet long, richly patterned in black and tan diamonds, restful to his eyes. He was thinking about the mystical nature of numbers. They tell the future, he thought to himself. He could immerse himself in spreadsheets and see all sorts of things—things that others couldn't fathom. I'm an interpreter, he thought. That's my real job, interpreting the numbers for Leon.

"Hey, Frank, she's a beauty isn't she?" Eric, the shopowner, stepped into the aisle beside him. "You should try her on for size," he said with a huge grin.

"I think I need a few more months at the gym before taking her on," said Frank, picking up on the jest. He knew the strength of a snake that size, and though he had handled some of the smaller reptiles, he'd keep a comfortable distance from this one.

Eric reached into the cage and stroked the giant. "I'd die for those muscles," he said. "Check her out."

Frank felt obliged to accept the invitation. He laid his hand firmly on the dense body sheathed in scales, then recoiled in surprise, a creepy feeling shuddering up his arm. The skin was loose. He shook his wrist and looked questioningly at Eric.

"She's getting ready to shed," he said. "Just came out of her opaque stage. Guess I should have warned you. In a day or two there will be some serious skin in there."

Frank wasn't sure if Eric was intentionally toying with him, but he was put off enough to make an excuse about getting back to work. His train of thought had been broken, and he was disgruntled. He'd been trying to figure out what his next moves should be. The meeting had gone well that morning. Leon had finally given him enough leverage to affect things the way he wanted to, but there were a few details still missing, and he'd hoped a few minutes with the snakes would give him some ideas.

It had taken him months to convince King he needed to toughen up at PRIMETEC, even after the bad publicity. He'd thought it would happen much faster, but Singer had been an influence on King. Frank had finally persuaded Leon to quit listening to her, but Helen was still a threat. It worried him. She was just too soft and she didn't understand the numbers.

Maria was exhausted by the time she finished her session. It was nearly five and she had been intensely involved for two hours, but she was stunned by what she'd experienced. Was it possible that one could lose a part of one's self and live for years without it? All she knew was that it seemed to make perfect sense.

The memory came back to her as vividly as if she were still six years old. She saw her father come home drunk that day, yelling and throwing toys across the yard. She grabbed her little dog, Penny, and ran around the side of the house to hide, but he came after them. When Penny growled and bared her teeth in a menacing manner the man became even more enraged. He grabbed the small dog and threw it aside. With a pitiful yelp it landed awkwardly on its neck and was forevermore silent. Maria's father was instantly filled with remorse. He hadn't really meant to harm her beloved pet, but the brutality of the incident would forever change him in his daughter's young eyes. When they buried her under a tree in the back, Maria took the bronze tag off her collar and stored it in her ring box. She hadn't thought about that for years. She wondered where the ring box was.

She was fully grown before she understood that her dad had lost his job that day. He was bereft and didn't know what to do. As an adult she could begin to understand, but what she was also learning was that part of her own being had left that day too, a part that was unwilling to risk her father's rage.

She glanced at the instructions Jason had given her for reflecting on their session. "Maria, now that we have retrieved this six-year-old part of your being, ask her three questions: 1. Why did you leave? 2. What are you coming back to help me with? 3. What, if anything, can I do or change to make you feel more welcomed?" As tired as she was, she would do the homework tonight. She was certain it was an important part of rebuilding her confidence on the job.

Checking her cell phone, she saw there was a message from

Mark. He had set a meeting for operations and wanted her to come if she could. "We need some fresh insights," he said. She was already booked and wondered if there was any help she could offer in lieu of attending the meeting herself. An inspiration struck. Jason Hand. In his short time on contract he had given her valuable support. She'd been thinking he could assist Mark as well, but hadn't had a chance to introduce them. She made a note reminding herself to do so before the meeting.

King stayed in Manhattan that night. He was too agitated by the events of the day to settle in the suburbs. It was almost as though he felt the city's pulse beating in synch with his own—the kind of restlessness that would have sent him into the club scene in his younger days. He decided to drop by a fund-raiser at the Met. It was to support an exhibition of photographs of European cave paintings. He would run into friends and maybe happen upon something interesting. He'd only been there a few minutes before he realized he wasn't in the mood for the schmoozing that came with the wine and cheese.

On his way out, a print caught his eye. It was a rare color shot of the striking "Sorcerer of Les Trois Frères," in France. That's how I feel tonight, he thought, like a wild man dancing in animal skins. He was on an ego high, feeling the power that came from having asserted his will that morning. He focused on the details of the painting. The dancer seemed to be wearing a mask and horns. An eerie feeling came over him; the image was posing a question in his mind: Am I wearing a mask? The moment of self-reflection felt like a pinprick, popping his heady mood. He grabbed a plastic cup filled with wine, downed it, and hit the street hailing a cab. Maybe there was something happening in the Village.

FOUR

Shaman leaves the lower world to bring the young soul home. He rises up on round drum sounds through succulent leaf layers. Then up again he rides the rhythmic tunnel to the middle world. Lost souls go blind-eyed through dust. The choking man now dances as though hung, his spittle casting forth, infecting all. He tries to wriggle from his stifling flesh while a spider weaves a web between his fingers.

Several days later, during the short walk from the parking garage to his office building, Mark couldn't get a clear grasp on how he was feeling. Edgy maybe, but not really nervous. He ducked out of the wind and ordered an iced coffee at the take-out bar, cool comfort on a hot morning. He mentally reviewed his outline for the department meeting at nine. It wouldn't be an easy one, but he felt confident he could charge his people up for the year-end push. He would start by giving out a little praise and then segue right into the bad news. It was never fun being the voice of doom, yet he was strangely unconcerned about what might happen.

That's new, he thought to himself. I don't really care. That's what this feeling is about—limbo. I've lost my edge. I'm not invested in what happens today. But as he dropped his cup into the trash and headed out again into the warm August air, a pain grabbed at his stomach. He buried it as best he could and continued at street pace, three blocks to the office.

When he arrived to prepare for the meeting, Jules, his tech aide, was double-checking the PowerPoint presentation. "It's all set, Mark," he said, tweaking the brightness on the screen. "Here's the new chart you wanted. I entered it as image number seven. Oh, there was a guy here looking for you, said he'd be back for the meeting. Jason something, I think he said."

"Thanks, Jules. Yes, he's a new guy whose been working with Maria in marketing. Some kind of internal consultant." Whatever that is, he thought as he checked the projected image. "I met him briefly the other day."

A surge of orange light teased the far edge of Mark's left eye. Turning his attention to the doorway, he found himself looking into a pleasant face and deep blue eyes. "I know I'm a little early," said Jason Hand. "Hope you don't mind."

"Oh no, make yourself comfortable. There's coffee on the table in the corner." Mark masked the slight irritation he felt at the intrusion. "I'm just finishing up a few details."

Jason sensed he had interrupted. To ease the situation he said, "Don't mind me, I know you're busy. It's just that I find it helpful to watch a meeting build from an empty room."

"I know what you mean," said Mark with a sigh of relief. I don't have to baby-sit him after all, he thought, and followed Jules out into the hall, calling for him to find a roll of Tums. "I think the milk was bad in my iced coffee," he said, overriding his concern that something else might be wrong.

The room soon filled with Mark's leadership team.

Muffled chatter rose and then fell when Mark stood to say, "All right, folks, we've got some work to do this morning, but first let's give Marion Crowley a big thumbs-up for her work on the new PSV prototype." Hearty applause and a few whistles signaled recognition of Marion's accomplishments. It relieved a little of the tension in the room, as Mark knew it would. He spelled out how she'd solved a tough design problem and made brief mention of her team members, then he moved on to the business at hand. "Let's get right to the point," he said, and began his presentation.

The first few charts clearly showed the serious nature of the situation. New products and product extensions in the pipeline were late; cycle times were too long for both the short and long term; and operations was on the line to bring out products faster. They needed higher quality and much stronger market acceptance. To most in the room, it was old news. They'd seen the same reports for several quarters, but there was considerable shuffling and coughing in the room as they noticed the unusually grave tone of Mark's voice. "So the bottom line is, for the third quarter in a row, we've missed our product development milestones and it's showing up as lost market share. We've got to find a way to reduce our cycle time in the short term, and create long-term growth with strong new market entries." He asked about timing on the current cycle and where the bottlenecks in new development were. "We've got to get this handled," he said and clicked forward to the next image, which was a bit of a surprise.

It was a simple chart of the company's current process for product development, something that would normally be thought of as elementary.

PRODUCT DEVELOPMENT PROCESS

	Conduct Customer Research	Design Product	Build Prototype	Beta Test Prototype	Manufacture Product	Rollout Product
Customer	✓					✓
Sales						✓
Marketing	✓					
Operations			✓	✓	✓	
Design	✓	✓		✓		
Finance						

Everyone knew there were problems, but they had expected the usual focused goal-setting and motivational jawboning. What was Mark doing? Going back to basics was fine, but did he really expect to motivate this roomful of veterans by starting at square one?

"You can't get blood out of a turnip." It was David Henley, a top manager in manufacturing, who finally spoke up. "There's no more time or money left to cut." His statements bounced around the room like a volleyball, as other leaders echoed it in their own words. Mark called for order. Flashing his laser pen at the chart, he led the group into a process for examining the six points one at a time.

Jason watched the meeting thoughtfully from his place at the back of the room. It was clear to him that Mark and his team were blinded by details. About an hour into the meeting, Mark seemed to catch on too. He wasn't inspiring the fresh approach he'd hoped for. He called for a twenty-minute break and prayed for a miracle.

Jason slipped out of the room and found his way to a quiet corner in an empty office nearby. He closed the door, pulled his tape player from his briefcase, and put the headphones on. He took a few deep breaths and formed his question: "What insight would benefit Mark's team at this time?" Not wanting to raise the curiosity of unexpected visitors, he left his blindfold in the briefcase, pushed play, and closed his eyes.

The drumming always soothed his mind and prepared him for his journeys. His imaginary pathway into the lower world was well-worn and comfortable. Off through the fields to the swimming hole where he had played as a kid. He took three deep breaths, then dived in. Down, down through a tunnel until he burst out in the forest, green, dense, and deep. He sought out the one power animal that always gave him great insight into business issues, Ram. Not the most exotic of his spirit allies, but always creatively practical, one foot in front of the other, balanced and persistent.

In his mind's eye, Jason glided just above the dense under-growth catching glimpses of Owl, Snake, and Mouse. Then his view opened onto a rugged mountainside, Ram's terrain. There he was, a mature mountain sheep with a healthy set of horns. Jason moved in close with his question foremost in his mind: "What insight would benefit Mark's team right now?"

Ram lifted his nose and started off on a thin trail that went only a short way and ended. He turned around and walked back. Jason understood what Ram was saying with his move: we're traveling down the wrong road—reaching a dead end.

Then Ram looked pointedly past Jason's right arm, butting his head gently to indicate that Jason should turn around. What he saw when he did was a railroad track that started at his feet and ran straight across an open expanse, its rails meeting at the horizon. Parallel tracks, he thought, more than one thing happening at once, parallel processes starting here and coming together down the line. Get the design team and the marketing team working in parallel with production and delivery. Involve every department that affects product development in any way at each critical juncture.

Next, a train appeared. Jason saw the back end of the caboose and assumed the train was traveling away from him, but it kept getting bigger, and he realized it was actually backing up toward him. Let's see, he thought, start at the end point—that would be the customer, yes, start with the customer. Get customers involved in the beginning and keep them involved throughout the whole process. He was always delighted by the unexpected ways his power animals gave their advice.

He turned back to Ram, gave a nod in honor of his wisdom, and glided away from the mountainside, back through the jungle, up through the tunnel, and into the fields where he had begun his journey. Opening his eyes, he found himself once again in the empty office. He turned off the drumming tape and took a moment to collect himself before reentering the hallway.

On the way back, he approached Mark, whose eyes were fixed thoughtfully on the meeting-room door. Jason startled him, and he reacted by holding out his open package of Tums. "Want one?" he asked.

"No thanks," said Jason, "but I'm glad I ran into you before the meeting started again."

"I wish I had more answers," said Mark.

"W-e-l-l . . ." Jason had a way of laying out the word that was both welcoming and leading. "It's a tough situation you're up against. I've had some thoughts. I'm not familiar with your operation, but—"

Mark interrupted his disclaimer. "Look, over the years I've come to know the value of an outside opinion. What's on your mind?"

Jason asked several skillfully targeted questions that led Mark into a mini-brainstorm. After a few minutes Mark summed up what they had covered: "So we work parallel tracks. Everyone involved meets to get started, then the teams work independently and meet again at critical points throughout the process."

"Sounds like a plan," said Jason. "How about including your customers somehow in the process?"

The idea immediately registered with Mark. "Maybe we should form a new kind of product advisory group, a sampling of our customers." His mood visibly lifted as he continued. "Instead of just doing focus groups and surveys at the beginning, we could get customer input every step of the way, and not just on design and manufacturing—on marketing and roll-out plans too. By the time the new product hits the market, we'd have a sure thing and our cycle time should be reduced. We'd have fewer false starts, less rework."

He was invigorated by the process as he built on the ideas Jason had sparked. Mark had the breakthrough he'd hoped for. "If we start with customers and work backward to the design phase, we effectively create a customer value chain as we go," he said with growing enthusiasm. "Start with the customer and work backward. . . ." Suddenly, his thoughts were like magnets pulling him toward the meeting room. How should I introduce these ideas? he wondered.

Jason watched Mark go and thought about Ram. He chuckled to himself. If Mark only knew! He smiled when he arrived in the room to find Mark and Jules busily reprogramming the presentation. Jules must be pretty good, he thought, when the display image finally came up. It was a new version of the same chart—the six points of product development. Only this time, it was filled with check marks indicating points of customer involvement.

CUSTOMER IN PRODUCT DEVELOPMENT PROCESS

	Conduct Customer Research	Design Product	Build Prototype	Beta Test Prototype	Manufacture Product	Rollout Product
Customer	✓	✓	✓	✓	✓	✓
Sales	✓			✓		✓
Marketing	✓	✓		✓		✓
Operations	✓	✓	✓	✓	✓	
Design	✓	✓		✓		
Finance	✓		✓		✓	✓

Mark opened a discussion on the amended chart. Everyone gave input until there was understanding and buy-in all around. By the time the meeting was over, even Henley was thinking of ways to get his people involved. He left the room wondering how he'd get comfortable with continuous customer input.

As the room cleared, Mark reflected on what had happened in the hallway earlier. He realized that Jason had given further definition to the thought he'd had at the executive committee meeting when he sensed that it wasn't the way they were executing their plays but the plays themselves that weren't working. He saw how expanding beyond operations and teaming up with the whole organization was the new game plan.

His excitement rose as it always did when he knew what to do next, but he paused, sobered by the size of the task he was taking on. I'll have to expand my influence, he thought, to build the broader team. Better be careful how I do that in the current climate. Instinctively, he followed the others into the hall looking for Jason, who was just approaching the elevator.

"Jason, got a minute?" he said. He moved closer and continued, "Those were some thought-provoking questions you asked me earlier. I don't know if you know it, but you saved my butt in there. If you're free for lunch, I'm buying."

Jason smiled and accepted. They settled on a time and place. As he said goodbye to Mark and stepped through the elevator door, Jason's suit coat caught a draft. For an instant, the lining flashed open, casting a brilliant rainbow across the elevator wall. He pulled the jacket around him, the rainbow disappeared, and the elevator started down.

FIVE

Like puffs of smoke the sonic beats ascend, drumming through countless cloud shapes. Shaman springs into the upper world, an endless expanse of blue. He sails with heartbeats open, free of ego, his questions begging answers meant to heal. He seeks a teacher, Maura, a bridging spirit breathing air and water, linking mind and heart. He finds her swimming deeply in darkness and splashing high to glisten 'neath the moon. Shaman asks, "Can I bridge worlds too?"

A question very like that was running through Jason's mind just before noon as he made his way to the restaurant: how to context the work he did to make it more accessible to people in business. In the past, he had positively impacted a number of business situations and people, and, as had happened this morning, he was always gratified and delighted by the results. But because he was concerned about maintaining his credibility in business circles, he didn't often talk openly about the methods he used.

His clients had, so far, come through direct referral—one adventurous person to another. It was a chain built of confidentiality, direct experience, and trust in him as a practitioner. His contacts were generally people who were sensitive to the human pain and suffering that often accompanied corporate life. They readily understood the efficacy of Jason's approach. He was at a juncture, though, where he wanted to offer his skills to a broader clientele, and he knew it would be a challenge to present them in meaningful business terms. Jason knew his considerable credentials from his corporate background provided him access. He had the track record and knew the language, but the shamanic journey and other practices called for nothing short of a leap of faith.

Jason's previous career as a senior officer in a large communications company had shown him again and again the folly of holding the bottom line as the only indicator of success for a business. He realized that while shareholder wealth always has to be a critical concern, the profit from which it is derived is, in reality, a lagging indicator. To manage a company by profit alone would be akin to sailing into reef-filled waters and steering the boat by facing backward and looking at its wake. His reasoning was that what is required for success is managing the leading indicators, one of which is the spirit and commitment of a company's employees. With the relentless pressure of achieving quarterly earnings, all too often concern for short-term profitability preempted the kinds of actions that would create and sustain employee loyalty. It was here that Jason believed he could make a significant difference.

Well, he thought to himself, I've got an opportunity here to try some things out with Mark. I'll test the waters and see how receptive he is to unconventional approaches. This isn't just an uphill battle, he thought, it borders on miracle-making, especially considering how uncomfortable most people are with any kind of change or new approach. He smiled to himself as he recalled a bumper sticker he had seen several days earlier: "Change is good . . . you go first!"

The Fifth Avenue Grill was humming through another busy lunch hour, the wait staff smartly clad in jeans and white starched aprons. They were greeting customers, reciting details on exotic concoctions, and opening premium brands of spring water. At a table near a big queen palm, Mark and Jason asked a few questions of their waiter and ordered. Then they ventured into a dialogue, continuing the friendly rapport they had achieved earlier in the day.

They talked sports and probed a little for common interests, telling brief stories on themselves for levity. Their salads arrived and they were well into them when Mark pushed back from the table uncomfortably. "I don't know what's going on with me. It seems like no matter what I order lately it doesn't agree with me."

"Hmm," said Jason. "You offered me a Tums at the break this morning. I thought maybe you were just a little tense because of the meeting."

"I probably was, but I was blaming it on coffee," Mark said. "Between you and me, I've been getting these pains for over a month now."

Jason had an impulse to probe a little deeper, but he didn't want to make Mark uncomfortable. "It's interesting how physical ailments often show up at about the same time as challenging life experiences," he said.

"What do you mean?" said Mark.

Jason reached for the saltshaker and said, "Would you mind if I do a little experiment here?"

"I guess not," Mark said, watching with curiosity as Jason

held the saltshaker up to the light and began to turn it slowly, gazing intently at the white crystals inside the beveled glass.

For a split second Mark thought he saw a wedge of bright violet light streaming from the shaker, but his attention was diverted as he heard Jason saying, "When you first started noticing the pain, was there anything unusual happening in your life? Some change . . . related to work maybe?" He seemed to look right through Mark as he set the shaker back on the table.

Mark's eyebrows pressed together and he heaved a weighted sigh. I barely know this guy, he thought, but he's zeroing in exactly on what's happening in my life. Without fully understanding why, Mark decided to confide in Jason. "Yes, there was," he said soberly. "For several months now I've been thinking about leaving PRIMETEC."

There was a respectful silence as both men took in what had just happened between them. They understood the level of risk involved when a confidence was shared with a business associate who was inside the same company. They both knew Mark could have just compromised his right to choose whether to stay or leave. If the rumor mill picked up on what he had just said, his personal sovereignty in the matter could become so much grist. He could be ground up and forced out, scripted as someone who wasn't loyal to the cause.

Jason tracked silently with Mark's thoughts, intuiting the impact on his new acquaintance of having breached an inviolate boundary. Finally he broke the silence. "I see. . . . Well, first let me say that I understand what a risk you've just taken by confiding in me. We don't know each other very well. I want to assure you that anything you say to me will be kept in strictest confidence. . . . Actually, confidentiality is a big part of my job description."

Mark was relieved. He had never met anyone who cut so

directly to the core of things. This was no ordinary business-man. "What exactly do you do, anyway?" he asked. "You don't seem like the average consultant to me!"

Jason eased back in his chair, a big, warm smile lighting his face. He shook his head just slightly and his gaze floated thoughtfully to the ceiling. "Guess it's time for me to confide in you," he said, shifting to direct eye contact. "I guess my offi-cial title would be something like Executive Coach, but that's really just jargon that gets me in the door for the real work I do. I don't try to explain my job to most people, but after our experience this morning, I don't mind telling you a little bit about it."

Mark's sense of adventure was mounting, "Sounds intrigu-ing," he said and waited for Jason to continue.

"Well, for some years now, I've been involved in the study of shamanism. Have you heard of it?" he asked.

"Isn't that some pagan religion or something?" Mark replied, his expression revealing a sudden skepticism.

"No," said Jason, "it doesn't have anything to do with reli-gion. It's a methodology for maintaining personal health and power. One of the goals of shamanism is to restore beneficial power while removing power that is harmful."

"What a concept," said Mark. "Seems like something we could use at PRIMETEC."

"That's why I'm here," said Jason. "But PRIMETEC is just one example. I've been in business for over thirty years, and I've seen the same power struggles again and again in company after company. I've come to the conclusion that power struggles are the single most destructive force functioning in business today. It's like an unacknowledged game that's being played, and the funny part is that nobody's winning."

"How's that?" asked Mark.

"Well, very often the guy at the top—I say 'guy' because unfortunately it still is usually a guy—who wields the power is like a warden at a prison. He's convinced he's got the advantage because he gets the big bucks and he has at least the illusion of control. But to keep his control, he has to be tough, and in the end he becomes a prisoner himself, locked behind a wall of force and fear."

"I guess I've had an inkling of that," said Mark, "but that's a great analogy. Sometimes I feel like the warden myself, and sometimes like a prisoner." He was studying Jason's face now, keenly interested. "So, where does the medicine man thing come in?"

"Shaman," said Jason gently. "We've tended to look at business as a machine. When the machine gets broken, we bring in mechanics to fix it. Most consultants fall into that category. They are called in to give their input on what's broken and apply their skills to fix it. Would you agree?"

"I guess," said Mark. "I could see that in the flavor-of-the-month phenomenon we've been experiencing for about fifteen years with consultants. A lot of different mechanics coming in with different tools and methods for fixing the machine when it breaks down, and with what result?"

"Right," said Jason. "Some people adapt and others try to, but most just bide their time until the new fad passes and then go back to what they were doing in the first place. Don't get me wrong, though. There are many business issues that can be impacted by consultants. But the way I see it, business is more than just a machine. It's a living, breathing organism that has a life of it's own." He was passionate. "And that's because it's made up of people who are organic in nature, not mechanical."

"You're right about that," said Mark. "It's the people problems that are the toughest to solve. I can think of six challenges right now in my department where people issues are at the core."

"Exactly," said Jason. He was still playing with the salt-shaker, turning it and moving it about, Mark noticed, recalling the moment earlier when Jason had seemed to purposefully gaze right through the shaker as he asked Mark the question about his stomach pains. He made a mental note to check that out later and brought his attention back to what Jason was saying. "So if companies are living organisms, the power game is a kind of virus that's infected those organisms, and it's running rampant."

"It's an epidemic," said Mark. "And are you saying you're like the doctor? Bringing the cure?"

"In a way," said Jason, "but I prefer to use the word 'healer.' There's a subtle but rather important distinction between the two. In our culture, a doctor is more like a mechanic, someone who is called in to make a diagnosis and fix what's wrong with the patient. A doctor might write a prescription or recommend surgery, more like a consultant. On the other hand, a healer or shaman helps heal the wounds of the past and reestablish a healthy internal environment where a virus can't thrive in the first place."

"That's fascinating," said Mark. "I think I understand . . . like what you did this morning. You didn't solve our problem, but you helped us look at it differently. And it looks like that could result in changing the environment we're working in. How did you get the ideas you shared with me during the break?"

"I used one of my shamanic techniques to gain access to them."

"What technique?"

"I found an empty office and borrowed it for a few minutes to make what's called a shamanic journey. It entails shifting into a non-ordinary state of consciousness. The place I journeyed to is called the lower world. I get there with the help of a drumming tape I always carry with me. I went there and spoke to one of my spirit helpers—it's called a power animal. Ram."

"Spirits! Sounds like pretty soft stuff to me!" said Mark. "No wonder you don't talk about it to just anyone. Was it like a séance you did?"

There it is, thought Jason, the woo woo factor. "No," he said lightheartedly, "in shamanism, 'spirit' doesn't refer to ghosts. For the shaman, spirit is defined as anything you see that has positive power when you are in complete darkness. We could translate that to mean anything that shines new light or gives new insight when there is confusion." He could tell he was stretching Mark's worldview. He moved back to basics. "Here's an example from business," he said. "Years ago when Goldwyn and Mayer decided to found MGM, they probably had a sense of what they wanted the company to become, like the world's best motion picture company or something like that. Right?"

"Yes," said Mark, "though I doubt they created a formal vision the way we do in business today. But, yes, I imagine it was there, implicit in what they were doing."

"Then, at some point," said Jason, "fairly early on, they adopted a mascot that would represent that vision of the company—do you remember what it is?"

"Yes, the MGM Lion, the king of the jungle," said Mark. "It's still their logo."

"Right, but in those days there weren't logos, really. The

idea of branding hadn't evolved to that point yet. The lion was more like a mascot, akin to what a sports team would have had."

"That's interesting," said Mark. "A little Madison Avenue history."

"I guess so," said Jason. "Anyway, the lion became a rallying point for the birth of a powerful company, and here's my point: it gave the business a kind of power. It was a power animal."

Jason was confident Mark was with him again when he said, "Well, it certainly has had staying power. It has to have been around for over sixty years."

"Exactly," said Jason, "and I'll bet that on more than one occasion that animal has re-inspired the leadership at MGM by providing a symbol for excellence during chaotic times."

"I see what you mean," said Mark. "It would be interesting to do a study on the animal symbols that have lasted over time. Remember the Flying Red Horse? Wasn't that Mobil Oil? Hey, I remember the animal even when I'm not sure of the company!"

"There are hundreds of examples in sports," said Jason. "The Denver Broncos, the Miami Dolphins, countless high school and college teams . . . and think of the Eagle and the Bear . . . and the Dragon. They immediately say America, Russia, China." He was having fun as he went on, "So what animal comes to mind when I say 'Merrill Lynch'?"

"A Bull," said Mark, in the spirit of the game. "But let's get back to your power animal from this morning. Is Ram like a personal mascot for you, then?"

"In a way," said Jason, "except that as a shaman I have a number of power animals I can call on for help. Ram is particularly good at giving me insights on business issues. I have others who help with other kinds of things. I even have a cow, and believe me that one really surprised me when I first came across her. In shamanism, we do a process called a power animal retrieval where we journey into an altered state seeking out an animal helper for ourselves or our clients. My first time, I was all psyched to get a really neat power animal for myself—I was thinking maybe a panther or an eagle, something with a lot of, well, power. So, this cow shows up! I can tell you I didn't want to accept it at first." Jason was animated as he continued, "This big, spotted, cud-chewing Bossy! It was very humbling, but she's been a great teacher to me. She's shown me a lot about healing through nurturance—not exactly the kind of thing I learned on the football field!"

Jason continued, "The helping spirits which watch over us believe that we humans aren't doing a very good job of managing things here on earth. Over the centuries we've lost touch with nature and natural ways of being. In the process, we've become more and more abusive to each other and to the earth."

Despite the intensity of his words, Jason's tone held compassion as he went on. "Power animals can help guide us back to a more respectful coexistence with each other and our surroundings. Children seem to have a natural sense of this with their affinity for animals. You know, how they spontaneously create imaginary animal friends when they feel lonely or scared."

Many questions were running through Mark's mind, and Jason patiently answered the ones Mark could put into words. He explained how a power animal was retrieved and brought to life in ordinary consciousness.

It was nearly two when Mark noticed the restaurant had grown quiet. He wanted to know more, but it would have to wait. "I'm not sure how to digest all of what you've told me," he said. "Could we talk again?"

"Sure . . . why don't we set up a time to meet in my office. It's a little different from most of the offices at PRIMETEC. We could do a power animal retrieval for you if you like," Jason said.

Mark felt a surge of excitement mixed with apprehension. They decided on the following Monday and were finishing up with the bill when he said, "One more thing. I've been wondering about the saltshaker. When you were asking me the question about my stomach pains, you seemed to be studying it. What were you doing?"

"It's called divination," said Jason. "It's a very simple shamanic technique. You ask a question in your mind, and then you reference an object and look for information that is pertinent to the answer. Normally you might use a rock or something from nature, but after doing divinations for years, I find that man-made objects work pretty well too."

"How did you know to ask about my job?"

"I didn't start with that. I started by asking, 'Where is Mark's discomfort coming from?' When I picked up the shaker and turned it on its side, at first the salt didn't move. It was stuck in a lump. That told me two things about your discomfort. First, something unusual was happening, because salt will normally move pretty easily in a shaker. Second, the discomfort had to do with being stuck somehow."

"All this from a saltshaker. How did you know I was thinking about making a change?"

"I knew that change was part of it because suddenly, for no apparent reason, the salt shifted on itself and fell to one side. The rest was easy—just human nature really. Your pains came while you were actively involved in your role as head of operations. So I guessed the change was related to work."

"Makes sense when you put it like that," said Mark. He was enjoying this. It was like a mystery novel, using subtle clues to do inductive reasoning. "Was Sherlock Holmes a shaman?" he asked with a wry smile.

"Could well have been," said Jason laughing. "I guess that might make the Hounds of the Baskervilles power animals."

The reference to mysteries reminded Mark to ask the one remaining question in his mind. "When you were using the saltshaker . . . for divination? Is that what you call it? . . . I thought I saw a flash of purple light come out of it. What was that about?"

Jason looked around the room and pointed to a row of decorative lights not far from their table. "Probably just the bevel of the saltshaker picking up the light from those lamps," he said, reaching for his suit coat. He was careful to keep it folded on the way out until Mark was well ahead of him. There were some things Mark wouldn't be ready to hear.

SIX

Fire crackles. Rattle and drum lie silent. Mask, staff, and cloak await the life that only Shaman gives. He passes an eagle feather through the smoke of cleansing sage. His space of solace clears of troubled memories and false hopes. It is renewed, a pure temple once again, where lessons can be learned and respectful intentions formed. Shaman hears the spirit Maura: "The teacher must wait for the student to come to him or the will to learn is not strong enough to guide the student into understanding and change."

Jason sat quietly in the dark. He'd been thinking about a shamanic ritual he'd learned, a process to help him become power-filled. He was preparing for his session with Mark, making sure he could bring the best of himself to the work. It was three o'clock and Mark would be coming any minute. He picked his way through a large basket, pulled out a sage stick and a rattle, and placed them on the table.

Like any shaman, Jason had his own demons to overcome, his own wounds to heal, and he was grateful for the guidance of his teachers. His passion for taking shamanism into business posed more than a little threat to his impeccable business credentials. He held an M.B.A. from Wharton and membership in several highly regarded business organizations. His patrician standing and sterling reputation had, for thirty years, opened the most prestigious doors in business. He was respected for his track record as an entrepreneur, but he was most highly revered for his unrelenting commitment to personal trust and individual accountability as the foundation of a successful enterprise. It was central to his thinking that numbers should serve a business, not the other way around.

At age sixty, Jason was haunted by the passing of values from his youth when the word "company" was almost synonymous with the word "family," and the owner or boss was like a parent providing for employees and fostering a sense of security. Inherent in that family model were the values of loyalty which went both ways, personal accountability, hard work, and goodwill. Jason had seen those values begin to erode in the seventies and virtually disappear in the eighties and nineties as quarterly stock values became the driving force in business, or new-economy companies created value based on promise rather than performance. Now there was little trace of the old family model left, and Jason agreed that wasn't all bad. Ultimately company-as-family had the same limitations that most conventional families have; all the power is at the top and the price of security is obedience and dependency—conditions that stifle the creativity required for business in the twenty-first century. Creativity, after all, can only be available in direct proportion to freedom of spirit and self-determination.

He was thinking to himself that it seemed as if many companies were saying, "We still want your obedience, but you can't be dependent anymore. You've got to fend for yourself, but you'd better do it within our strict guidelines." There were a few organizations that had been able to form new virtual families in which an important part of the parental or leadership role was to support every individual in achieving his or her full potential. In such places, entrepreneurs blossomed inside and creative teams flourished, but there were still far too many companies where individual genius was ignored or even stifled and creativity was more feared than celebrated.

As with so many of the great cultural changes of the twentieth century, the old organizational mores had fallen away, but the new ones hadn't formed yet. There were giant voids, and to Jason they were like gaping wounds that would have to heal before the new forms could establish firm footing. He believed that shamanism could help heal those wounds.

He had discovered shamanism in the process of recovering from wounds of his own—physical as well as emotional wounds inflicted when he suffered a heart attack without warning in his mid-forties. Faced with the fragile nature of his own mortality, he had begun a journey of self-discovery that ultimately led him to a workshop on shamanism. Once his body mended, he continued to be very active in business and could only devote part of his time to his new exploration. It took years for him to learn the shamanic ways and begin to see the world through new eyes. Once he did, what he saw everywhere around him was the pain of others, many others, and nowhere was it more prevalent than in the back halls and elevators of corporate America, where shocking stories of betrayal and despair were cautiously whispered.

Vivid in Jason's mind was a different picture: people walking those halls and riding those elevators with pride and a sense of belonging. He began slipping shamanic wisdom into the business presentations he gave, and he saw that people were hungry for what they offered. Finally, he decided to make the healing of business his primary focus. He resigned from VoiceCom, the highly successful global telecommunications company he had helped to grow from three customers and a garage that served as a manufacturing plant. At first, he targeted medium-sized firms that were big enough to have people and spirit issues but not so conservative as to reject his approaches out of hand. He fantasized that one day he would be called by a giant company like Dell or 3M to facilitate a shamanic journey in the boardroom. Or how about Merrill Lynch? They could find Bull and bring his spirit back to the firm—Bull, the ancient symbol of green pastures, love of home, and consistency of thought and deed, sometimes to the point of stubbornness. Jason was more than curious to know what Bull would have to say about the bull market that had dominated Wall Street in the late nineties.

Jason's mind came back to the present. He was surprised to find himself at PRIMETEC. It was of a size and stature several steps beyond the other companies he'd worked with. If PRIMETEC was receptive to shamanism, it would be a great model for other larger companies. It was a temptation to get invested in creating a success here, but he knew better. As a shaman, running his own agenda was unthinkable. He must trust the process and keep his own need to succeed out of the equation. His teachers and power animals would always create the most appropriate results regardless of his own preferences. I will need Leon King's buy-in, though, he thought, and from what I've heard, that doesn't sound too likely. Okay, don't go into scheming here. Remember, the teacher must wait for the student to come to him. Introducing shamanism to business happens one person at a time. I've made some progress with Mark. It'll be interesting to see how the session goes today.

It was nearly ten after three when Mark arrived. He'd had trouble finding the office tucked away in its remote location. It was part of a small lab facility that was rarely used. Jason thought it would be perfect when he learned it was available. He wanted to be out of the mainstream of activity. The hallway to his office was stark, with bare concrete floors and plain plastered walls, a vivid contrast to what Mark saw as he opened Jason's door.

"Hey," he said as he entered. "This is great! How did you set this up? You must have smuggled these things in!"

The room was as warm as the hall had been cold. The floor was stained a deep amber and laid with a beautiful ethnic rug. The walls were faux-treated as aged, dark adobe. The furniture in the room was casual and cushy, the only possible desk a small table set with an African straw mat and several curious artifacts. On the walls were artfully arranged pictures and objects, and in one corner was a cabinet that housed exotic totems from all over the world. In the center of the room, near a comfortable sofa, was an Indian drum so large it could have been a table, but there was a rawhide-covered mallet lying on top of it—it was clearly meant to be played.

Jason was warm too in his welcome. "Come in," he said. "Make yourself at home." Mark was a little embarrassed, remembering his own agitated response to Jason's arrival at the ops meeting. His chagrin lasted only a second, though . . . he was swept up in the enchantment of the shaman's space.

It was almost as though the room were alive, the way it cradled the experience that ensued. Jason offered tea or soda, Mark chose the latter, and after a bit of small talk, they moved to the purpose of the session, the journey to retrieve a power animal.

"Let's start with a little orientation to journeying," Jason said. "A journey is a way to open up to the possibility of getting help. When we journey to retrieve a power animal, it is to allow the essence, or spirit, of the animal to assist us. For instance, I might come across Otter in a journey, and that would mean to me that I need to lighten up a bit, bring a little more playfulness into my life."

Mark responded as most people do to the idea of Otter—with a warm smile.

"You see what I mean?" Jason said. "The very word 'otter' elicits a warm, friendly thought. So the 'power' of Otter has something to do with playfulness and lightheartedness. Other animals have other unique identifiable 'powers.' Elephant has the power of strength and royalty, and Deer has gentleness and innocence. Do you follow me?"

"I think so. You're saying that power animals are more than just mascots; they're specialists in a way, power specialists."

"That's a great way to put it," said Jason. "Shamans call them spirits, and that can be a little confusing, because the meaning is different from what the word 'spirit' means in a religious context. It's more like 'the spirit of . . .' kind of thing. Otter brings the spirit of playfulness; Elk the spirit of strength and nobility. So we're not talking about ominous ghostly entities that have enormous powers to manipulate people and things. We're simply meeting energies like playfulness and strength so those energies can be more available to us."

"Why do you call it a retrieval?" asked Mark. "That makes it sound like it's something you had at one time and lost."

"Exactly," said Jason. "The story that shamans tell is that

you are born with a power animal who will protect you in your life. Somewhere along the way, because of an intrusive or destructive occurrence, the animal might leave you. This lessens your power and may leave you open to illness, or chronic depression or some such affliction. The idea is that by retrieving the power animal, you reestablish the protection and it's easier to avoid or overcome the affliction."

Mark said, "You mentioned at lunch that you had several power animals. Does that mean I could have different ones, too, to help with various afflictions or problems?"

"Yes," said Jason, "Each power animal has a unique type of guidance to offer based on its characteristics. For example, if your eyes were giving you problems, Eagle might visit you. Eagle is known for extraordinary vision. In human terms it is said that an eagle could read a newspaper at five hundred feet, but physical eyesight isn't the only issue that might summon him. He could also bring new perspectives and new vision to other parts of your life."

"That's so interesting," said Mark. "I was telling a friend just yesterday that I've been wishing I could get away and hibernate for a while; then this morning I had a dream about a bear."

"It could be that our discussion about power animals the other day was enough to start your unconscious mind thinking about them on its own," said Jason. "But it doesn't mean you have to physically hole up in a cave. Bear is also symbolically about introspection and your ability to find the inner resources you need for your survival."

"Well, that fits," said Mark. "I've been thinking I need more time for self reflection."

"Is that what you want to focus on for your power animal retrieval today?" asked Jason.

Mark's answer went to humor once again, "No, I'd probably get a horse and ride on out of here!" he said.

"Well, you're getting the idea—Horse does represent travel," said Jason. "But since you mentioned him, you might want to know he also stands for power and freedom. And not all power animals are glamorous. Snake, for example, is often rejected by people at first until they learn that its shedding its skin represents transformation. And, of course, when you look at the caduceus, the medical symbol, it has two snakes intertwined up a staff. Here snake represents healing."

Mark nodded knowingly, and they talked a bit more about his purpose in doing the power animal retrieval. Jason was surprised when Mark said he wanted a mascot for the retooling project he was orchestrating.

"Well, we certainly could retrieve a power animal for the team," he said.

"I've thought about it a lot since our lunch," said Mark. "I'd be fascinated to have my own power animal and I'd love to do that at some point, but I'm feeling a lot of pressure right now on the job. As I pull the team in from different sectors of the company, I need a way to unify the players. Many have never worked together before. I liked what you said about getting an animal symbol that could inspire a group, and I think it could really work."

Jason had been hoping for an opportunity to do a group power animal retrieval in a serious business setting. This would be his first, and with Mark's enthusiasm, it had the potential of working well. He felt a little twinge of excitement and checked himself. Okay, he thought, be the shaman. Let go of your agenda and set the stage for Mark's experience. Expectation is the enemy of spirit.

"I always like to burn a little sage to clear the space before journeying," he said. "Would that be all right with you?"

Mark was game; he didn't know exactly what he was getting into, but he was comfortable with Jason, and he watched with curiosity as the shaman carefully lit the bundled sage and waved it gently, sending a pungent stream of smoke throughout the room. "This is something some shamans do to clear away any negative energy," he said. He snuffed the sage out in a large abalone shell. "I'm going to make a little noise too," he said, and he shook a gourd rattle toward each corner of the room. "This will summon the positive spirits to support our work.

"For a power animal retrieval," he said, "you will journey into what we call the lower world. This is just a place where your journey will take you, and for most it is similar to being in nature. Technically, you'll be entering a nonordinary state of consciousness. You start by visualizing an entrance into the earth, something familiar to you, like a tunnel, cave, or swimming hole, something you've actually seen and are familiar with. I often use the pond where I swam as a kid. You don't need to tell me what you choose, just have it in mind as you start the journey. We'll have you lie down here." He gestured toward the sofa and pulled a length of cloth from his pocket. "I suggest you put this blindfold over your eyes to help you keep your vision turned inward. Just as a point of interest, 'shaman' is a Siberian word that means 'one who sees in the dark.'"

Both men positioned themselves for the journey, and Jason continued, "I'll begin drumming and you can just let the drumbeats carry you through whatever passage you've chosen and into the lower world. Just trust whatever you see."

Mark was fascinated and a bit skeptical. He felt a little embarrassed, but he was up for it. "So, I'm just going to start seeing things?" he asked.

"That's the way it usually happens." Jason's manner was serious yet very relaxed. "Just assume that whatever you see, feel, and hear is completely real. The less you question what you're experiencing, the more impact it will have for you. Try to approach the process with respect and an appreciation for the world you'll be visiting, the world of nature. Once you're in the lower world, you may start seeing various creatures. You want to watch for possible power animals. They are always friendly. They won't frighten you or try to hurt you in any way. On occasion you might see a creature that makes you feel uneasy. It's not likely that will happen to you, but if you do come across something that feels at all ominous, just go on by it."

"You make it sound so real, it's a little spooky," Mark said with a hint of tension in his voice. "Is it dangerous?"

Jason remembered the answer his teacher had given when he'd asked the same question: Yes, if you don't do it. But he chose a less pointed answer for Mark. "I've never heard of anyone being in danger. You are in control, Mark. If you see anything you don't like, just go around it or stop the journey and come back. To do this you can just open your eyes and *poof!* the journey is over. You are always in complete control. I don't think you need to worry, though. It's usually just as easy as a walk in nature."

Mark wanted a little more reassurance. "Do you have to get certified to do this kind of work?" he asked.

"I've done years of training, but no certification . . . no. A shaman's credentials are in the results he produces. In a sense it is his clients who certify him." Jason paused and asked, "Are you ready?"

Then he added some final instructions. "You'll know when you see your power animal because it will appear four times. It might show up in different forms, like a picture, a statue, or a toy, or as an actual animal. When this happens, you've found your power animal. If you still have doubts, just check it out by asking, 'Are you my power animal?' Well, in this case, 'Are you the power animal for the project?' or something like that. You'll get a solid yes if it is. Then you want to bring the animal spirit back with you, so, in your mind's eye, gather it into your arms, hugging it to your heart. Embrace it and bring it back. I'll give you about ten minutes to journey, then I'll signal you when it's time to come back. Here's the signal." He made a distinctive pattern with the drum. "Just enjoy the journey. If you see something you don't like, go around it. You can end the journey at any time by retracing your steps or simply opening your eyes. Any questions?"

Mark said no and stretched out on the sofa, tying the blindfold over his eyes. Before Jason started drumming, he said, "Since you're journeying for your whole team, take a minute and picture the different people who will be involved." Seconds of silence followed, then the drumming began. It was louder than Mark expected and it took him a minute to adjust and relax again; he was glad that Jason's office was in such a remote place. Presently, his mind focused on an old mine shaft he'd once seen out West. It had seemed to have no bottom to it. He visualized himself standing at the entrance, and then jumping in, going down the tunnel into the dark, deeper and deeper. Okay, he thought, here we go. I can't believe I'm doing this. His mind chattered on. What if I don't see anything? Everything's black. Then, as if by magic, he found himself coming out of the dark tunnel and into a bright open space. Wet ferns tickled his ankles, and he rocked a little to balance himself on the spongy moss beneath his feet.

He was in a tropical rain forest. There were birds, hundreds of them, flying, singing, nesting, and an alarming fly the size of a grapefruit. It came right for him, buzzing loudly around his head. Just pass on by . . . he heard Jason's instructions repeating in his head. Now this is fun! he thought as his mind carried him through the fresh green landscape. He saw a deer running off through the trees. There was a raccoon, too, and a rabbit. He was eager to see if any of these would appear again as his power animal.

His eyes fell to a pathway that opened ahead of him. He saw movement. A pure white rabbit hopped quickly into the dense underbrush. Mark spied something shiny on the ground. It was a brass button, with the image of a wolf's head molded in relief. His eyes darted about, alert and eager. In the distance, he heard a cry like a dog baying at the moon. He moved in that direction, keeping to the path, and soon noticed a piece of blue-and-gold cloth snagged on a tree. It was an old Boy Scout bandanna. Printed in one corner was another wolf's head. Wow! he thought. Maybe Wolf is our power animal.

He heard the howl again, off in a different direction from before. Turning his head toward the sound, he saw the trees open onto the sky, and there, formed out of clouds, was a whole family of wolves frolicking in the blue. He was entranced, gazing at them in wonder. Then his attention was drawn to a large shape on the path ahead. He squinted to see it better and took several cautious steps forward. There, camouflaged by dappled sunlight, was a magnificent timber wolf, standing calmly, waiting for him. What am I supposed to ask? he thought. The words tumbled through his mind: "Are you the power animal I'm looking for?"

Though Wolf was silent, Mark had a keen sense that the answer was definitely yes.

Mark wanted more, much more . . . conversation, pictures, verification, proof! Wolf studied him for several seconds as Mark collected his thoughts. Then, as though standing outside of space and time, Mark opened his arms and invited Wolf in. He took him to his own chest to carry back to the waking world. He turned to go and realized that the steady drumbeat was breaking into a different pattern. It was Jason signaling to him what he already knew, that the journey was complete.

Mark found himself a little reluctant to wake fully into ordinary consciousness. Once back, he removed the blindfold and rested a moment, a sleepy look in his eyes. He was refreshed. "Wow," he said, staring off into space and shaking his head slowly. They talked about the journey and what Mark had experienced. Jason asked, "What does Wolf symbolize to you?"

"Well, I've always been fascinated by them," said Mark. "I've seen several shows lately on the Nature Channel about wolves being reintroduced into the wild. I think it's great they're doing that, but I guess a lot of people aren't too hot on the idea. What's your take on it?"

"Wolf is a very powerful, positive spirit," said Jason. "He represents personal power and a willingness to be open to new ideas. Wolves are family-oriented; they mate for life, and they're very loyal and protective of their own. They have definite, predictable group rituals, but a single wolf is strong by itself too. Wolves demonstrate a perfect balance between personal sovereignty and group process."

Jason and Mark were both struck by the appropriateness of Wolf as the symbol for the team. "Each person needs to be strong as an individual and yet feel like part of the family," said Jason. "It makes a lot of sense."

"I can't believe how perfect it is," said Mark. "Is it always so right on?"

"Absolutely," Jason answered. "Sometimes you can't see the fit right away, but it always makes sense over time. . . .

Remember I told you at lunch how power animals like to be a part of ordinary reality? That is, our world?"

Mark nodded, "You said they like to come out and play!"

"Right," said Jason. "You can help Wolf come into PRIMETEC just by giving her your attention every day. Get some pictures of her or figurines to put around the place in plain sight. And when you get your team together, introduce Wolf as the mascot for the project. You don't have to tell them where she came from!"

"Do you think they'll get it?" asked Mark. "It seems like wolves have a pretty bad reputation. They're always the bad guys, like the Big Bad Wolf—you know, he blows down pigs' houses, eats grandmothers, and chases little girls around the forest."

Jason picked up on where he was going. "Then there's the whole wolf thing about men," he said. "Men who chase after women. And there's the werewolf. Most people have ideas about wolves that are pretty negative. It will be important to bring that up when you introduce Wolf. You might have a group discussion, ask what people think about Wolf, and get the negative ideas out on the table. I have some books that explain the positive symbolism of different animals. You're welcome to borrow them and read up on the positive energy of Wolf."

Jason completed the session by encouraging Mark to record his journey in writing. "Get yourself a journal or notebook," he said. "The more credence you give to the experience you've just had, the more powerful your Wolf mascot will be for your team. If you're like most people, you'll probably start noticing wolves everywhere, in shop windows, magazines, on TV."

"Maybe I'll rent *Dances with Wolves* over the weekend!" Mark said, not sure if he was joking or serious.

SEVEN

High upon the mountain, Shaman sits alone while moon and sun and stars mark off the days. He moves between the worlds outside of time. A dark transformer snakes between his dreams, her body filling up the spaces. No head, no tail, no end in sight—gigantic diamond patterns gliding on tubular flesh. Shaman hears the chaos of the world below, and knows the time will come to share his gifts of healing there. For now, he calls his wisdom home and waits while dead skins fall away.

It was late in the day and Maria was still going strong. It's October already and I've been so absorbed, she thought. I hardly remember September. She recalled her weeks of hard work both on the job and in her personal life. She had fully reclaimed the lost six-year-old part of herself, and it had given her renewed vigor and optimism, almost as though the vitality of the child had come back to her once the painful memories were acknowledged and expunged. She no longer felt threatened by Leon's rough edges, no longer associated him with her father in his moments of anger. Each Thursday as she reported in, she felt stronger and more competent.

She was coordinating quality control on a wide range of marketing details and working hands-on with the customer team. She enjoyed the balance between people-focused activity and administrative time alone. She'd never been so happy in her work. I'm healed, she thought to herself, envisioning a charismatic preacher, hands waving high.

The marketing department had been ignited and was purring along like a Mercedes, smoothly and precisely. They were ahead of schedule on the current rollout and making great progress on new product plans, coordinating well with operations and sales. Maria's recovery was part of the equation, but the big change came from the resurgence of Mark's team. It had been dubbed "the Pack," and everyone involved had a wolf of some kind in his or her cubicle. Some were toys, some pictures. Maria had a delicate gold wolf charm hanging from her bracelet. One of the computer geeks had taken to wearing a ball cap with wolf ears poking out the sides and a Disney watch with the Big Bad Wolf on it. At exactly noon each day, it beeped and he let out a chilling howl to signal the lunch hour.

The wolf power animal and subsequent theme of "the Pack" energized Mark's team and brought it together, releasing a level of enthusiasm and creativity that had long gone underground. But there was much more to the operations turnaround. Careful planning and disciplined execution became vital team values. Three different customer advisory groups were formed and used effectively, each for a different part of the operation. Meetings at which critical decisions were made always included nondepartmental people who would be affected by such decisions. And the laborious task of process improvement had shaken much of the waste out of the system.

With all the Pack activity going on, it wasn't long before

Leon King's curiosity was piqued. He was seeing wolves every-where, and knew they were tied to a surprising turnaround that was showing up in his weekly review meetings with Mark. His curiosity got the better of him finally and he asked Mark, "You've explained the uptick in results you've been getting at our weekly meetings, but how does this wolf thing fit in?"

"The wolf is a mascot," said Mark. "A symbol for the new team approach we've instituted." He pulled out the operations chart he'd been carrying around since the ops meeting six weeks prior. It was smudged and torn around the edges. "Here's what's up," he said. "We've created an integrated team. Every department that affects product development in any way is involved, and we've brought our customers more directly into the process too."

He went on to give details, with Leon nodding approval at each turn. "Very good!" Leon said finally. "How did you come up with this idea? You were under a lot of pressure, and this is definitely out-of-the-box thinking."

"To tell the truth," Mark replied, "it didn't come from me. It came from Jason Hand. He sat in on our team meeting back in August. Things weren't going very well, and during a break, Jason started asking me questions. He . . . well, for want of a better word, he finessed me right into a completely fresh way of seeing what was going on."

"Jason?" said Leon. "Isn't he working with the marketing department? What's so special about him?"

"It's hard to explain," said Mark, "but he has a way of com-ing up with solutions like you wouldn't believe. I don't want to overstate this, but he's like a magician."

This was the most positive moment Leon had experienced in months. He actually got a smile on his face, and it was contagious. By the time Mark left his office he was grinning too. Things were working, and Mark was feeling the pride that every coach feels when he sees his team executing a winning strategy.

In contrast, John Conatello was losing ground—fast. There were problems at home: Kevin had been out of school for a week with chicken pox; Liz's schedule was off; there'd been plumbers at the house for three days trying to find a nasty leak; and John's mother was coming at the end of the month. Everything was hitting at once. He managed to cover his foul mood at home in the evenings, but he wasn't interested in even trying to hide it at the office.

John had gotten a slow start after the big meeting. He was at his best when he had a lot of room to move, and the pressure he felt around him was constrictive. But eventually he had gotten up to speed. Now, weeks later, his sales force was on the street and sales were up, but he was getting complaints from the old-timers about the added requirement that they push their customers on past-due accounts. It was out of character for sales people to dun their customers for money. They loved to sell and they liked to please, but it was demeaning to act as collection agents. John sympathized with them; chasing receivables would be a push for him too. He was caught in the middle, his team griping at him from the street, and Frank Farratt breathing down his neck.

John was pacing in circles, wondering how he could resolve the situation, when the phone rang. It was Leon asking about the top sales situations. John happened to have updates sitting on his desk, and he leafed through them, answering all of King's questions, but he felt himself getting agitated in the process. He's really going to keep right on top of me week after week, he thought angrily. It's enough that my weekly report is due in two days, and I'm still grappling with receivables. He finished the call fuming.

Seconds later, Helen called about the district manager position in Cleveland. They had hired an experienced young woman weeks ago, but Helen was worried because the Cleveland-based teams were mostly cocky veterans, all guys, and the woman was having trouble asserting her authority. "I told you she'd come unglued," said John gruffly.

"You told me if she had the qualifications on paper to hire her. I advised you it was against my better judgment," said Helen.

A rocket went off for John. "Why are you calling me?" he yelled. "We can't afford to change that position right now. All I can do is tell her to toughen up and get the job done!"

Helen very deliberately removed the phone from her ear and held it where she could look at it while she decided what to do. She'd had several confrontations with John in the past few weeks, and her first impulse was to yell back at him, but she thought better of it. She brought the phone back to her ear, forcing composure. "Great," she said flatly and hung up.

John was itching for a fight. He was infuriated that Helen had left him hanging. He was about to call her back when Eleanor, his assistant, stepped in to say, "Frank Farratt's on his way down."

"I'm not here," John growled. He slammed the phone down and charged the door, nearly knocking Eleanor over. She spun around to see him disappear from the suite, and began searching for words to cover for him when Frank showed up.

Frank was pushing hard to bring his numbers home. He'd clamped down on accounting and was seeing results, but the invoices sent to John's people were being paid as slowly as catsup flows from the bottle and he wasn't happy about it. In his mind, he had a clear picture of the rows and columns that made up his projections for the quarter, and he wanted the final reports to match them—exactly. His confidence in his ability to turn cash flow around was bolstered by the fact that King was giving him more and more authority every day. He'd even been sent down to Wall Street last Friday to meet with the Goldman Sachs people. Unfortunately, in his desire to paint a bright future, he had relied too much on the picture in his mind and not enough on the facts. Simply put, he'd overstated PRIMETEC's position. Now he was trying to cover his tracks, and John was in the way.

Frank was undeterred when he found John was out of his office—he grilled Eleanor instead. Where was John? When would he be back? How much time was he spending cleaning up receivables? His probing violated Eleanor's sense of loyalty. Each answer she gave was terser and less informative. Frank was seething when he left the office. John's not doing a thing, he thought to himself. He's not taking this seriously.

He called accounting to see where receivables stood and learned that there were two sales regions that didn't seem to be taking the mandate to heart. That's it! Frank said to himself, heading for Leon's office. He charged in unannounced and blurted, "We've got to put the screws to Conatello." A heated discussion ensued as Leon tried to calm him down enough to deliver the full story.

"I'm not happy to hear this," Leon said when Frank was finished, "but I'm keeping a close eye on John. I spoke with him just moments ago and he seems to be doing his job."

"He's not bringing those accounts in. He's let the whole thing slide in some of the most critical regions. We're losing precious time." Frank didn't want to admit that he'd gotten ahead of himself with Wall Street. He pressed to keep the focus on John. "I'll chase him down and get his report, but you've got to back me. If he's asleep on this thing, we've got to come down on him."

Frank was smart, and he was sincere in his dedication to PRIMETEC, but he didn't have King's commanding style or his considerable self-control. In the Chinese *Book of Changes* it says, "An inexperienced man struggling to rise easily loses his own individuality when he slavishly imitates a strong personality of higher stature." It perfectly described what was happening as Frank identified more and more with the power and status of his boss. The problem now was that he did have King's ear.

The positive feelings of being a CEO in control that King felt after laying down the law in his August meeting had dissipated rapidly as the onus of follow-up and enforcement mounted over the weeks. He found in Frank a willing deputy and relied on him frequently to monitor infractions, while he himself focused on the weekly report meetings, which were, by their nature, brief and rather formal. Consequently, King was increasingly isolated from the human element at PRIMETEC. He had a clear sense of how well his people were performing, but he had no idea how they were feeling. His posture might have been adequate for a CEO under normal conditions, but Leon's own actions had pushed PRIMETEC into a volatile state of change and he wasn't performing his leadership role— as change master. Nowhere was this truer than in the decision he was making at the moment concerning Frank's request to handle the Conatello debacle. It constituted a terrible lapse in judgment when he sighed finally and said, "Okay, you carry the ball on this, but keep me informed." He might as well have armed Frank with an AK-47 for all the subtlety with which he would now proceed.

Over the next few days, John was flooded with calls. There was the normal traffic: Maria wanting his blessing on her schedule for the rollout; Cleveland calling to complain about the sales manager situation; Liz needing details about the household plumbing. But, as a direct result of Frank's inflated sense of control, the accounting department called several times every day pumping John for information on receivables, his field sales people were harassed in the same manner, and Frank himself made it a point to call several times a day asking about various additional details. If John had been short on time and temper before, he was now running on empty.

It was Friday, about thirty minutes before his weekly report meeting with King. John was pulling information off fax and e-mail and picking at Eleanor while she tried to assemble his report at the last minute. Then his cell phone rang one more time. "Conatello here," he said fiercely as he switched it on.

When John heard the sound of Frank Farratt's voice for the third time that day, he lost it. He hurled his cell phone into a bookcase. It bounced off *The Seven Habits of Highly Successful People* and landed in a creeping Charlie plant. He could hear the garble of Frank going off at a distance as he grabbed his jacket and headed for the street.

So when Frank showed up at King's office for John's weekly report meeting he was astonished to find John absent. "I want him out of here!" he demanded, as though he had the authority to make it happen. "He's gone over the line. He disappeared on me earlier this week and now he's blowing you off. He needs to go!"

Leon hated the position this forced him into. He was shocked by what he was hearing, but he wasn't about to fire John summarily. "I'll give Helen a call and check out our position," he said, trying to put Frank off.

But the words were barely out of his mouth when Frank jumped in: "Let me handle it."

The last thing Frank wanted was for Leon to get an earful of Helen's considered opinions on the matter. She would defuse the situation and undermine Frank's position. He was more than gratified when he heard Leon say, "Find out if she knows of anyone in sales who could step up, and get the initial facts on a possible severance package. See if you can get me something by tomorrow morning. If you can't catch me at home, try me on my cell phone or leave the basics on my voice mail."

Leon watched Frank go. That should keep him busy, he thought. I need time to think about this. He'd planned for the weekend to squeeze one last overnight sail in if the weather continued to hold. It would give him the time he needed to get perspective.

Frank pounced on Helen like a cat after a sparrow. "John's out of here," he said. "Leon wants to know who could step up in sales, and he wants preliminaries on a severance package." He was visibly gloating. "It's confidential, of course, but John's a loose cannon and he's going down."

"Leon's asked for this?" she questioned, alarmed and dubious.

"Yes, what do you think? I'm making it up?" said Frank.

There was little evidence in Helen's mind to suggest that Frank wasn't following orders. She'd seen John acting out—she was mad at him herself—and Leon had been in the habit of passing responsibility to Frank on a number of things lately, but Frank's unexpected assault impacted Helen in a way that was surprising even to her. It's a crummy deal, she thought. Leon's bailing out and Frank is a pompous fool. John's been a handful, but Frank's been riding him hard and he's had a lot of other pressures too lately. It's just not right to cut him out without a complete review and probation.

She had the feeling that she was sitting in a house of cards that was about to collapse. She didn't like the glimpse she caught of herself slipping on the rubble about a month down the road. She asked her assistant for several files, and when they came in, she handed them to Frank. "You can review these yourself," she said resolutely. "And while you're into the severance material, keep me in mind too, because I'm not sure I'll be sticking around. You can be sure that I've got the system down and I'll take good care of myself in the process. I have the names of a few first-rate attorneys who will be happy to assist me, and I'll be giving their numbers to John as well."

Frank had a split second of lucidity when a bolt of fear zipped through him, but the intoxication of power quickly overrode it as he realized that he might have managed to kill two troublesome birds with one pounce. He feigned concern and flaccidly asked Helen to remain with PRIMETEC, but he didn't wait for her response. He took the files and left, masking a growing sense of personal opportunity.

EIGHT

The middle world is dry as dust. Shaman passes through. The choking man still dances, swaying in the wind, but now his eyes are open. His hands search for understanding and find the gift of breath. He listens, so Shaman speaks: "The future lies in what's already working. Water the seeds that have sprouted." These words are truly spoken, but they won't be heard today. The music of a ringing bell spirits them away.

There are rare instances when the separation between worlds dissolves and the dreams of people come together into a set of interconnected experiences. Leon King was about to enter such an instance as he woke to the sound of a bell buoy clanging off the port bow of his sailboat. She was dragging her anchor and had drifted to within a few yards of the marker, which had been silent in the calm water until it was tipped by the wake of a passing trawler.

Leon leaped from the cabin, pulling on his sweatshirt to combat the chilly morning air, and started the boat's small engine in time to avoid colliding with the buoy. It would take only minutes to reanchor the boat at the place chosen the night before, but they were to be out of time by minutes. For in the quiet of the dawn, his eyes soothed by the gray light, Leon's thoughts returned to the nightmare he had just escaped.

He'd been trapped in an eerie, existential waiting room, bound in shrouds and dangling from a tree, his feet frantically dancing on thin air. He could still feel the soreness in his throat as he cried out to a passing traveler, his words choked off as though he'd been hung. When he reached overhead to grab the noose, the choking stopped and he realized he was sitting in a child's swing, and that he'd been choking himself with his own hands.

The traveler had a friendly face, one Leon was certain he'd seen before, but he couldn't remember where. He almost felt as if he had shared the dream, as if it was the traveler's dream, too, but for him not a nightmare, just a curiosity. Leon looked down from his dream swing and saw Frank Farratt below, struggling as he tried to hold on to a giant snake that was shedding its skin. He knew in some strange way that he was the snake, or at least a part of it. The traveler said something to him, but his words were lost in the tolling of a church bell. The swing heaved violently from side to side, waking him.

It was Sunday morning. He had set out from Stamford the day before on course to Mystic Harbor, taking advantage of the exceptional Indian summer that was gracing the East Coast. It was like a last gasp of warmth before the icy winter months ahead.

Despite the fair winds and pleasant temperature, Leon had sailed through a horrendous storm of his own making on Saturday—a deluge of messages and emotional reactions. It started with the question in his mind: Why had John Conatello blown off the meeting on Friday? It was out of character for John, and Leon wasn't convinced Frank had told him the whole story. His suspicions were heightened when he sailed close to shore later in the day and picked up a message from Frank on his cell phone. "John never showed up again yesterday." Frank's voice was matter-of-fact. "It looks like terminating him is going to be pretty simple. And I have some surprising news: Helen's thinking of leaving. I guess she didn't like the idea of firing John. Personally I think she's overreacted, but maybe it's for the best in the long run if she leaves too."

Leon was no longer listening as Frank justified his reasons for not reporting these startling facts sooner. Any one of the things Leon had just heard would have distressed him, but hearing them in tandem and so long after the fact was terrifying. He felt PRIMETEC slipping from his control and into a deep crevasse. John had disappeared, for some mysterious reason; Frank had overstepped his authority and led Helen to believe that John was getting the ax without warning; and Helen had done the only thing she could do to keep her self-respect under the circumstances—she had threatened to resign. Leon's terror turned to fury centered on Frank. I'll blast him, he thought. That conniving creep. What a mess!

Just then the wind shifted and the sails began to luff. It's part of the magic of sailing that it directs the mind unexpectedly back to the simplicity of the elements. Leon's state of agitation mellowed some as he focused on trimming the sails. The rocks along the Connecticut coast trailed by, and he thought to himself, it's as if my crew has run aground . . . and I've been down below with my nose in the charts. How could I have missed the fact that we were so far off course?

Suddenly his mind flooded with hindsight. I've given Frank far too much latitude, he thought. He misinterpreted my meaning; I only meant to keep him busy for a while and he already had John out the door. I guess I shouldn't be surprised. He was pretty set on the termination yesterday. I wonder if Frank started all this by setting John off somehow. I should never have given Frank so much authority. . . . And Helen—I haven't seen much of her lately, but she's been one of the best friends I've ever had. I can't believe she's been pushed to the point of leaving.

Leon tried to reach both John and Helen, but he couldn't connect. He tried again a bit later and picked up a message from Helen. It was an earful . . . six months' worth of frustration downloaded into a three-minute explosion—words he couldn't believe she even knew. What on earth had been going on? How could things have gone so far awry? He wondered if he should sail back to Stamford and try to make contact. After some deliberation, he decided to stay his course. The sail might continue to clear his mind and give him a fresh view of things. All afternoon he sailed through painful memories until he felt obsessed by them like mad Captain Ahab. At sunset when he dropped anchor, he had spiraled into depression. He uncorked a bottle of fine port and drank himself into a deep wine sleep.

Now, in the light of the new day, he saw the meaning in his nightmare. He had been choking himself off from the world around him, doing a dance of power, false power, his feet never hitting the ground. Frank had been in the trenches, aware of what was going on, but incapable of handling it all. Too much change, too much pressure, too few personal resources.

Leon felt ashamed, sick at heart. It was excruciating, but he was almost relieved to be feeling something—anything, even remorse. He remembered an adage that spoke to the moment: "He who will not heed will be made to feel." Helen tried to tell me, he thought . . . months ago.

Jane Peters was working security on the main floor at PRIME-TEC that Sunday. It was midafternoon and she was watching the monitors when she noticed that one of the cameras seemed to be acting funny. A gentleman had gotten into the elevator on the ground floor and was on his way up. For a second the monitor cut away to a pattern of strange-colored snow. Jane did a double take and the snow was gone; the man was alone in the elevator, adjusting something under his left arm. Moments later the door on her right opened and Jason Hand approached the desk to sign in, his briefcase in one hand and his jacket rolled tightly under the other elbow. "I'd better have a look in your briefcase," Jane said. "Can't be too careful when things are slow."

Jason knew this would only take a minute. The case was ordinary enough, like a million others, plain brown leather with shiny brass clasps. But when he opened it, Jane's eyes flashed to his, questioning. The inside looked like a plush display case. A cushion of deep blue velvet was custom-formed around a set of exquisite artifacts. On the left was a black-and-white Hopi thunder rattle made from a gourd. Next to it was a leather journal tooled in Celtic symbols. On the right was a drumstick that looked to be of Oriental origin, inlaid with bone and mother-of-pearl. Beside it lay a small mask, overlaid in brilliant patterns of brightly colored beads in the manner of the Huichol natives of northern Mexico.

"Well," said Jane, "I can't say this stuff looks dangerous, but it is a little out of the ordinary. Are you in the art business?"

"No," said Jason, "but my work does have a creative element to it." He closed the case and went on his way with Jane's blessing. He wasn't sure why he'd brought the totem objects with him—in fact, he wasn't exactly sure why he'd come in at all. That morning he'd gotten a mental picture of himself sitting in his space at PRIMETEC, and he knew enough to trust the images that formed in his mind. He decided to come in, determined to see what was prompting him.

The office was dark. He set the case on the table and lit a few candles, then he opened it thoughtfully. His eyes were drawn to the mask, his symbol for one of his master teachers, Nayarit. He took it out and placed it in the chair next to the couch. He reached for his small cassette player, unfolded his blindfold, and lay down to begin his journey. He intended to travel to the upper world, in search of Nayarit. Instead he was drawn to the middle world, where he came upon a figure he had seen before, the choking man. It is a principle of shamanism that you never give assistance to a person without his or her express permission. The idea is that it is not up to you to decide what people might need or when they should receive it. So Jason was always cautious when he came upon strangers in the middle world. This time, however, the choking, dancing man called out to Jason as he passed. His eyes, which had been closed before, were open, and the man seemed to be awake, maybe for the first time.

Jason watched as the choking man released the hold he had around his own neck and reached into the air above his head. At that moment, Jason recognized the man. It was Leon King, and he was crying out for help. Then a rare and wonderful thing happened. Jason felt the presence of his teacher Nayarit. He spoke these words: "The future lies in what's already working. Water the seeds that have sprouted."

The words were masked by a bell ringing. It puzzled Jason and brought him back to normal consciousness. Despite the interruption, he knew he'd gotten what he was looking for. He sat in the candlelight for some time, reflecting on the journey.

Occasionally a shamanic teacher will appear spontaneously if his help is needed. This can happen even to someone who doesn't know about shamanism. Indeed, it had happened to

Leon King in his dream that morning. Now Jason had seen the dream through his own inner vision. Even though he was quite used to such happenings, he continued to be amazed at the laser-sharp precision with which his journeys often illuminated the waking world.

He suddenly understood why he had been drawn to the office this afternoon. He was here to learn that Leon King was ready to meet him, open-minded and trusting enough to benefit from shamanic practices. Jason reflected on the teaching he'd received in another recent journey: *The teacher must wait for the student to come to him or the will to learn is not strong enough to guide the student into understanding and change.* Leon had somehow mustered the will to face the demons that held him prisoner.

Dreams and visions come to people in different forms, even those that are shared in the spaces between time. Not all dreams come in sleep—not all visions in a shaman's journey. Sometimes they make themselves known in broad daylight, a part of consensus reality. These are, perhaps, the most difficult to identify and translate into deeper meaning because they appear to be outside one's self rather than a mirror of one's own inner condition.

Tribal peoples from all parts of the globe have learned to read these happenings for their meaning. They sometimes call the process reading sign. A raven flies over a burial site punctuating a moment of grief; the rains come after the kachina dance, foretelling the joy of the harvest. One Sunday afternoon Frank Farratt struggles out of a taxi with a rolled-up rug he bought at a street fair on the Avenue of the Americas. It is a foot taller than he is, wrapped loosely in plastic. The plastic wrap catches on the cab door casing and tears away, and the rug springs open onto the filth of the street, smudging forever its diamondback pattern in rich black and tan.

NINE

Two hands float, gently searching. The darkness will be found. It aches and sweats the body, to draw attention down. Down into deep waters where spirit leaves no trace, where hurts and harms assemble hiding in the night. Confusion and illusion make deception wily prey. Shaman finds his way there, feels his way along, and coaxes the alien creatures out into the sun. They burst from light exposure; the healing work is done.

Viewed through hindsight, the events leading into Monday morning at PRIMETEC look like choreography in modern dance, chaotic yet inspired, the moves of each dancer carefully designed and performed to perfection. As a series of human exchanges unfolding over several days, those same events look more like a soap opera brought to you by the rumor mill.

After leaving the office on Friday, John went home and turned off his phones. He ranted for an hour to Liz, then put on his jeans and helped her clean up after the plumbers, preparing the house for his mother's visit. He was feeling justified in claiming the time at home, and more than a little relieved to have the whole weekend to pull himself together.

Helen did decide to resign and left a letter explaining her decision on Leon's desk. She then went directly from PRIME-TEC to an attorney's office, where she left the paperwork required to review her severance status. That evening she called Maria at home. "I'm beside myself," she said. "I desperately need to vent and I wanted to be the first to tell you the bad news."

"But things have been going so well," Maria jumped in, assuming the call meant her own job was at issue. "My meeting with Leon this week was great, and I—"

"It's not about you, Maria," Helen interrupted. "It's about me. I've resigned."

Static and the whisper of a voice bleeding from some other remote conversation were the only sounds on the cell phone connection for several seconds as Maria absorbed what Helen had said.

"Are you still there?" asked Helen.

"Yes, but I don't understand. What happened?"

Helen tried to remain calm as she told her story, but she was bursting with unexpressed rage. It leaked out as fresh anger does, ugly, raw, and uncontrolled. Leon must be out of his mind. He'd given Frank the authority to fire John. Frank was an ass. How could he even suggest they terminate John without warning? It was an inconceivable betrayal. Nobody was safe. She wasn't going to wait around to be next. She'd seen this coming for months. King had lost control. Why hadn't he listened to her? The supercharged story went on and on.

Maria heard only the first few sentences. Her mind was in a fury of its own. Would she be next, despite the recent success she'd been having? Had all her hard work over the past months been for nothing? Was there nothing one could count on? No one? She was suddenly consumed again by the past she had been trying to disgorge. She was the child once more, traumatized by the unexpected explosion of her father's rage, her world abruptly shattered.

Helen had unintentionally drawn Maria into hell's fire with her. When she realized it, she shifted her attention and spent the last few minutes of the call reassuring Maria that her own job security was intact. She hung up feeling worse than when she'd called. She'd distressed Maria and gotten no empathy for her own crisis. The anger in her grew with renewed vigor until, overnight, it festered and finally exploded in the message she left Saturday morning on King's home voice mail.

In the space of one short day, Leon's momentary abdication of responsibility had grown to catastrophic proportions and come back to him as a raging bonfire of righteous anger. In a quiet, passive way, he had lost control Friday morning by deferring to Frank. He had acted inconsistently, unwisely—setting off a chain reaction that wreaked havoc throughout the leadership of his organization. Such is the insidious potential of precipitous, inconsistent behavior when practiced by people in positions of power. The more power, the greater the potential for cascading devastation.

Fortunately, as a result of the personal journey she'd been on, Maria had some understanding of how inconsistent authoritarian behavior produces such chaos. She had learned that it can sometimes reignite childhood memories we carry, each of us—memories of dire moments when our formative will was crushed under the force of a teacher's abrupt anger or a parent's sudden change of mind. In those long-past moments, our child's eye witnesses the all-powerful adult, the stable force of our universe, alter our world for reasons we cannot comprehend. If the trauma connected to the change is great enough, it can induce fear or even terror. Children are protected from emotional obliteration in such moments by an internal defense system that allows them simply . . . to forget. But the fear remains unexpressed, lodged instead in the child's emotional memory. Like a forgotten land mine, it lies buried under the sands of consciousness, sometimes for decades, until a similarly charged moment of effrontery detonates it and it blows up. A proven and loyal performer worries about her job security. A full-grown man heaves his phone into a bookcase. A seasoned employee walks out on the job incensed by what she's been asked to do to keep it.

Soap operas rely on these knee-jerk emotional reactions to drive their ratings because we all identify with them, if not consciously, then unconsciously. When we assume ourselves to be above such drama, it is almost always because we are in denial about our own humanness; we are strutting like tourists down the beach that was the minefield of a bygone war, oblivious to what lies just below. Sooner or later something triggers us, something with enough weight to penetrate the sand cushion and detonate the deeper truth of our vulnerability.

We are wise to acknowledge our humanness, explore our personal weaknesses, and identify the triggers that fire them. We are safer then when we find ourselves in situations such as the PRIMETEC cascade where leadership has distanced and lapsed into inconsistency. We can protect ourselves from those who would find, in our moments of vulnerability, openings through which to advance their own positions in the power game, as Frank had done that morning.

Maria's momentary collapse on the phone was more the norm in human beings than the exception. What was exceptional was her ability to recognize, in the moment, what was happening and take responsibility for her own emotional well-being. She could feel the land mine going off and at least attempt to manage its effect, eventually restoring her equilibrium. It took only moments after Helen's call for her to regain full control of herself.

No longer in a state of panic, Maria felt a wave of regret at having been so self-absorbed. She wished she had been more sensitive to Helen's plight. As a business leader and a friend, she was aware of the impact her choices and actions could have on the people near to her. She knew about the importance of compassion because she was in touch with her own need for it. She tried calling Helen back to make amends. No answer.

In the confusion of Helen's diatribe, she'd neglected to mention to Maria that John still didn't know about his impending dismissal. So, late Saturday morning, steeped in innocence and motivated by good intentions, Maria called him to offer condolences and support. "I just can't believe they're letting you go," she said hesitantly after warming into the conversation.

She might as well have smashed him in the face with a two-by-four. He was numb. "What?" he said, his lips barely able to form the word.

"I heard you were laid off. I . . ." The reality of the situation dawned. "Oh no," she said, "you didn't know?" She tripped over her words. She was so sorry. She'd thought he knew. She felt just terrible.

Finally she grew still and the two of them listened to nothing, each hoping the other had a way out of the situation. Finally, John said in a faint tone, "It's not your fault, Maria." Pause. "I've got to go." Click.

He stood immobilized except for the automatic swivel of his head, back and forth, back and forth, his eyes changing focus as he searched his mind for a way to make sense of what he'd just heard. They just wouldn't do that, he thought. Would they? Surely he wouldn't be hearing this for the first time here . . . at home . . . on the weekend. There was some mistake.

Part of him wanted to believe that, but it wasn't long before his thoughts turned on him, presenting grim evidence to support what he'd just heard. He certainly wasn't on top of his game. The receivables were a nightmare. He'd disappeared on Frank twice in a week and blown off his meeting with King. Yes, they could be firing him. The monotonous swiveling turned into a hapless, vacant nod.

He tried calling Leon at home to get a reality check and learned he was gone for the weekend. Sailing. That bit of news bled the last breath of air from John's already deflated balloon. This is all so important to King that he's taken a leisurely sail up the coast! he thought. Either he's an unbelievably callous jerk or . . . or an inveterate coward.

On Sunday morning, Frank Farratt's stride was long and brisk as he made his way down through Central Park. He always enjoyed his Sunday walks, adventures through the never-ending variety of the city's weekend moods. Sometimes he happened on a parade or celebration, all color and crowd. Other times, like this morning, the city was quiet, an eerie void, but there was usually a flea market somewhere near Central Park South. He headed that way with a bounce in his step, following the sound of music that echoed through the concrete canyons. His mind was on automatic, toying with the numbers, the beautiful PRIMETEC numbers.

The Avenue of the Americas was blocked off from the park, south for several blocks. It was alive with booths and hawkers as Frank wandered through. For over an hour, he rummaged among racks of T-shirts, CDs, and other merchandise. He was beginning to tire when he came upon the rug seller and the diamondback carpet. Once it was purchased and rolled for portage, he realized he'd better catch a cab right away. He wasn't going very far on foot with it. Too long. Too heavy.

Once he was in the cab, a flood of concerns inexplicably set upon him. He wondered if he was really rid of John and Helen. He worried about whether he was going to be able to make good on his boast to Wall Street. Don't be silly, he said to himself, I only fudged a little, and it worked out okay last time, didn't it? The press had no way of knowing I deflated the numbers when they interviewed me for the article about Hawkins's resignation last year. It had to happen. King was getting too soft. I had to wake him up, and a dip in the numbers always gets his attention. I never dreamed it would make the *Wall Street Journal,* though. But that wasn't my fault. In a way, pumping the numbers up now is just an adjustment to balance things out. Ah, I'll come out of this smelling like a—

The cab door opened onto the rancid alley behind a fish kitchen. Frank reached to cover his nose and the rug slid to the pavement.

It took King most of Sunday to sail back down the coast to Stamford. He was a knot of contradictory feelings, anxious on the one hand to get his hands into the tangled mess at PRIMETEC and sort it out, and thoughtfully sobered on the other, the result of hours of painful soul-searching on the water. Once the boat was safely tied in its slip, he called Helen.

She made no bones about the fact that she had no interest in talking to him, but he did persuade her to listen while he tried to explain himself. When reason had no effect, he turned to emotion, ending up finally with pathetic cajolery. She is *really* upset, he thought, a swell of panic forming as he searched for one more point of entry.

"Look, I'm telling you I've been a complete jerk here. Can't we sit down and talk this through? I'm prepared to do whatever it takes to make it right." No response. "Please, Helen, just answer, would you? I'm running out of material here. You have every right to be upset, but . . ."

He was getting nowhere. "Okay," he said finally, "here's my invitation: I'm going to do my best to put things back on track. I'll call a meeting early this week, the whole team, and we'll get things sorted out. I would like you to be there." No answer. "In the worst way, Helen. Just think about it, will you? You don't have to give me an answer right now. Just think it over, okay?" He waited. Dreadful seconds passed. "Helen?"

Finally, through a dense fog of resistance, he heard, "I'll think about it." That was all.

Helen . . . John . . . Maria . . . Mark . . . Frank . . . the names were scrawled on blue memo-pad sheets, spread out across Leon King's desk. It was early Monday morning and he'd been pushing them around in different patterns for nearly an hour. Helen, he thought to himself, tapping the name absently with his finger. I've got to set up that meeting and hope like heck she'll come. He slipped her off to one side as though to table his distress. John . . . I don't blame him for taking off Friday. I need to get him in here today and make sure he's okay. Wonder when he'll get in this morning. Maria . . . she might have some help for me, or Mark, maybe. Frank . . . Leon had been tempted to tear that one up. It was hanging off the far edge of the desk. Pure justice if it sailed off and under the desk, he thought, lost to the cleaning crew.

He had come off the boat Sunday afternoon certain about one thing: he didn't have a clue about where to start in repairing the damage at PRIMETEC. He'd slept fitfully and taken the first train into the city, arriving at the office early enough to be the first person in the building. That's not like me, he thought. I must really be grasping at straws. He slid "John" in circles and reached for his coffee mug. Empty. As if on automatic, he was up and out of the office, making his way to the coffee bar, his mind still engaged, teased by a faint memory of something he'd heard—something about watering seeds that had already sprouted.

The soft rattle of the plastic spoon stirring a half pack of sugar into his coffee punctuated the stillness of the room. Had there been more activity, he might not have noticed the faint blue glow that suddenly appeared down the side of his white mug as if it were bathed in Christmas lights. At the same moment, the water cooler gurgled behind him and he looked around to see a gray-haired gentleman soaking a tea bag in hot water.

The man looked up and said, "Good morning," studying him thoughtfully. "You're Leon King, aren't you?"

"Yes. Do I know you?"

"Let me introduce myself," the man said, extending his hand. "I'm Jason Hand."

Leon was struck by . . . well, he'd have to say, by the man's presence. Not just his physical appearance. There was something else about him, an easy comfort. Jason. He tried to place the name and said, "Are you sure we haven't met?"

"We've rubbed shoulders a few times," said Jason with the hint of a smile, "but no, we haven't been introduced. I'm an internal consultant. Maria Martinez brought me in to help out in marketing."

"Oh, yes," said Leon, making the connection. "You're the guy behind the wolf pack thing."

The comment had the ring of a compliment, and Jason acknowledged it, saying, "My associates and I just gave Mark and his team a point in the right direction."

Leon was staring now, another spark of recognition. He looks like the guy in my dream, the traveler, he thought. He was there when I was hanging from the tree. King's brain might have been evolving right then, as he tried to cross-match fact and fantasy. Maybe there's something to that, he thought. Maybe this guy has some help for me. "What kind of internal consulting do you do?" he asked.

"Anything from executive coaching to critiquing a business plan."

Leon was curious. "What do you mean, executive coaching?"

"Well, I'm sure, as a leader, I don't need to tell you that sometimes people at the top get a little isolated. . . . You know, lonely at the top and that sort of thing." He went on to explain that his job was to be a neutral, reflective agent who could help a business leader access a more complete, objective view of things. "It's my experience that able leaders have keen insights about most situations. It's just that sometimes they can't access them. It's my job to help establish the connection."

Leon pressed for more information. How did Jason do that? Was he like a shrink? How did the wolf thing fit in?

Jason did his best to answer under rapid fire, but he knew he'd need to slow down the pace of the conversation if he was going to convey the responses he felt the situation warranted. "My approach is rather unusual," he said. "You could get a better feel for it if we could sit down at some point when you have time to talk."

"How about right now?" said Leon, thinking to himself, I'm here looking for answers. Why not? "Come on into my office." He motioned for Jason to follow as he strode down the hall. His mind raced on. I forgot about the notes on my desk. What will he think when he sees them? How can I talk about this mess to someone I hardly know?

King went straight for his desk, and whisked the blue sheets into a pile. Jason asked calmly, "Working on anything in particular?" He knew King had the feeling he'd left himself vulnerable somehow, and sought to assure him there was no need for concern.

Leon was at a critical juncture; he could feel it in his bones. The fear that had been running him for months demanded that he back way off his current position, shut up, and regroup. But a more compelling voice spoke clearly in his mind, saying: "You've been looking for a fresh approach. Here's one right in front of you. What are you going to do?"

TEN

Nine Shamans sit in circle, holding the world gently, with awe and reverence. They wait—the sacred drumming begins. One stands, he sings his song, begins his dance. He swings and spins, swoops and jumps, allowing himself to become power-filled. Then he passes on the wisdom of the ages to soothe the world of men. "The new leader has the heart of a healer. He earns the right to benefit from the power of those who follow him by fostering their well-being."

The memo-pad sheets in King's hand became an animated flipbook as he riffled through them absently, his eyes both searching and holding. "It's like you said," he confessed to Jason finally. "I feel isolated. I've got a huge mess on my hands, and . . ." He hesitated, questioning his judgment. "And I don't know what to do." His words caught up in a cough, demanding a sip of something wet. To free his hands, he stuffed the pile of memo sheets into a magazine he'd left open on his credenza. He closed it now and set it on his desk, took a sip of coffee, and said, "Have a seat," motioning toward a comfortable-looking chair facing the desk. He sat down in his own chair and sank back, pressing his hands together, fingertip to fingertip, as though to claim a moment of reflection.

The short silence that followed was broken respectfully by Jason. "It would be my privilege to assist you if I can," he said. "Why don't I tell you a little bit about how I work and you can decide for yourself if you want to know more."

King was relieved as the focus shifted away from him. "Great," he said.

Jason drew in a deep breath. He released it silently and slowly. "I'm what might be called a corporate shaman," he said, watching King carefully. "I work in organizations to renew company spirit." He was tracking every subtle change in Leon's expression, assessing, second by second, the effect of his words on the powerful, yet troubled man. "I'm guessing that if you feel as much at a loss as you've just said, PRIMETEC ... may have lost its spirit."

Leon was stunned by the implied finality in Jason's words and put off by their strangeness. He tensed his eyes and asked guardedly, "What do you mean by 'spirit'?"

"Well," said Jason, "let's start with what it isn't." He was on familiar ground now, words he'd said a hundred times in trainings and healings. "'Spirit,' as I'm using the word, is not religion. It isn't ghosts, and it's not alcohol. Actually, what it is is so individual to each person that for me to try to define it for you would be to risk excluding your own unique experience."

Though he was comfortable, he knew that Leon was not, and he offered a bridge. "Let's look at it another way. Can you recall a time when you felt engaged and committed? A time when you were so caught up in what you were doing that you were oblivious to time? When you knew without a doubt that what you were up to was important? And that your way of doing it was right?"

"That's a no-brainer," said Leon. "It's when we started the company. It was so exciting, working the bugs out of the product, getting our first order. Everybody was customer-oriented because we didn't have any customers. And it was just so much fun. Everybody did everything—that needed to be done. There weren't any battles over turf." His face brightened, then almost instantly paled as he flashed on how far away they were now from those early days.

It's like he's thinking he might never feel that way again, thought Jason. He waited for several long seconds, then said, "That time, your start-up days, were full of spirit. Does that help you with what spirit is?"

"Yes," Leon said. "I see what you mean. It's almost like a special kind of positive energy." Another wave of bright memories passed over his face.

Jason was very careful, very wise, as he moved the dialogue gently forward. "I take it things have been a little different from that lately."

Leon's head nodded heavily. He didn't speak.

"Mind if we take a closer look?" asked Jason.

"I guess that's why we're talking." It was the first of many answers that ensued, as Leon conveyed to Jason the history and current scope of the challenges at PRIMETEC. Once he'd described the situation, King concluded by saying, "I'm afraid morale has been dropping for over a year, but I guess that executive committee meeting in August was the critical juncture."

"What was the mood of that meeting?" asked Jason. "How do you think people were feeling? What was going on?"

King was obviously chagrined as he described the August meeting. He was realizing as he spoke how truly dismal it had been, and he was more than a little embarrassed as he saw for the first time the large part he had played in making it that way.

"I can see you're not happy with the way it went," said Jason when King was done. "Would it be safe to say it didn't come from a spirited place?"

"It certainly would," said Leon. "I think we could actually say it was dis-spirited. I was angry and everyone else was on the defensive. We were all like pouting children. And I'm afraid it was mostly my fault. I just wasn't listening. I guess I was a real jerk!"

"Don't be too hard on yourself," said Jason. "I'm sure you had your reasons for acting as you did. The question is, what do you want to do now?"

"I want to turn things around," said Leon without hesitation. "Two of my best people walked out on their jobs Friday. Helen Singer is a dear friend, and she may not come back. And I'm not sure how much of a mess I've made with John Conatello. I need to act right away, but I don't know where to start. What do I say to them? How do I even assess the full extent of the damages?"

"If we put it in terms of spirit," Jason said, "on a scale of zero to ten, zero being none and ten being maximum, like when you started PRIMETEC, where would you place the level of spirit at PRIMETEC right now?"

"I can tell you where Helen would put it," said Leon, making a zero with his fingers.

"So Helen would say no spirit at all. Do you agree with her?" Jason wanted to clarify where Leon himself stood.

"I'd like to think it's at least a five," he responded, "but I don't have a lot of evidence to support that. It's a pretty unhealthy situation."

"Hmm," said Jason. "Interesting that you would use the

word 'unhealthy.' It brings us full circle—back to shamanism. The life purpose of a shaman is to heal sickness of spirit. We have all sorts of healers around us—physicians for the body, psychiatrists and various therapists for the mind and emotions. A shaman could be thought of as a healer for the spirit."

Leon heard Jason's words, but was rapidly withdrawing his attention. He was exhausted and a bit overwrought. *This isn't going anywhere*, he thought to himself. *This guy's a little too far out for me.*

Jason sensed what was happening and changed course. "I'm sure if we thought about it we could score PRIMETEC in the middle somewhere on the spirit scale. It would be interesting to take a closer look, but I've got a few things I need to attend to this morning. If you'd like, we could continue our discussion another time."

"Sure," replied King, his response driven more by politeness than sincerity. Jason found his way out, and Leon reached for the magazine and the stack of blue sheets. He turned them over to find Mark's name on the top of the pile. Just then, the phone rang.

"Leon, this is Maria." Her voice was hesitant, anxious.

"Yes, Maria, what can I do for you?"

"It's about John," she said abruptly., "I'm afraid I've made an awful blunder." She went on to tell him about the phone calls, the one from Helen Friday night, and the one to John on Saturday. Once he had the facts, King hung up the phone shaking his head. *If ever the child in his complex psyche was crying out, the moment was now. What on earth is happening here?* It bawled, desperate in the realization that things were far worse than expected.

Where was I? he thought to himself with a greater sense of urgency. He reached once again for the blue memo sheets. As he did so, his eye was drawn to a quote enlarged amid the text columns of the magazine. It punctuated an article he'd been reading on Friday morning before things started unraveling.

Today's business leaders are reinventing everything but themselves. Unless executives realize that they must change not just what they do, but who they are, not just their sense of task, but their sense of themselves, they will fail.

Tracy Goss
Executive Consultant

The message was bold and impeccably timed. There was no way Leon could ignore the relevance it bore to his own situation, and it cleared his course of action. He needed answers. Jason Hand might have some, but he wanted to check the man out more carefully. Mark Steed would have good input. Leon dialed his extension.

"I can't recommend him highly enough," said Mark, "but I gotta warn you he'll pull you way outside your comfort zone."

"He already did," said Leon. "He was here in my office a few minutes ago talking about spirits." There was a moment of shared amusement on the line, but Leon continued his inquiry with serious intent: "But you think his approach is valid, right?"

Mark assured him that he did. He told of his own encounters with Jason, going into some detail about the operations meeting and the insights Jason had elicited. He talked freely about the wolf pack program but touched only briefly on the saltshaker lunch and his power animal retrieval experience. He knew he didn't have the words to explain divination and the shamanic journey process to his boss. After about twenty minutes of conversation, Leon asked for directions to Jason's office. Moments later he was headed for that remote corner of the building.

He arrived in a state of agitation. "I want to talk a little more," he said, cloaking his mood. "Could you make some time right now?"

Jason wasn't particularly surprised to see him, but he took a moment to put a few things in order, a delay designed to give Leon a few moments to settle down and adjust to the surroundings.

King looked around the room. This isn't a business office, he thought to himself. What kinds of things take place here? Hanging over the window were three intense-looking masks with painted faces and feathers fanned out for hair. It's like some kind of museum, he thought, listening to the music that droned rhythmically through the space. His own mood was a stark contrast, his mind jumping about on pure adrenaline. He was definitely out of his element, he knew, but there was something enticing here, a certain promise of repose.

"All that spirit talk seems pretty weird to me," he said when he had Jason's attention again. "I'm not sure I understand yet what you do. Just how do you work with spirits? Is it like using a Ouija board?"

"I could try to explain it further," said Jason, "or we can do a simple process that would give you a firsthand experience. Would you be open to exploring a little?"

"Right now, I'll try anything," said King, almost meaning it.

Jason knew there was groundwork to lay. "First we need to set the stage," he said, "by examining some of the basic reasons why spirit has such a hard time flourishing in business today. Let's start by taking another look at your start-up days. Tell me, what was the primary goal of your team at that time?"

"Well, getting into business," said Leon. "Establishing our customer base, bringing in good people."

"And what exactly happened when you did those things?" Jason probed.

"We would celebrate. It seems like we had champagne in here every other day toasting some new milestone." He reveled in these pleasant memories again.

Jason was identifying with every word and said lightheartedly, "So would it be fair to say that you were feeling good?"

As he nodded yes, Leon had the look of one who was deciding to trust a wise new mentor for the first time. Then Jason asked, "And when you think about being at PRIMETEC now, what happens when you get an order or bring in a new hire?"

Leon responded without hesitation, "We hardly notice. Our attention is on bringing in the numbers." The seriousness of his response landed with a thud, the weight of the world settling once more on King's shoulders.

Jason took note, but continued respectfully with his questions. "And what happens when you bring in the numbers? Do you toast them with champagne?"

The tone of King's answer was as terse and dry as its content. "We pass out a few accolades, figure out what we could have done better, and start focusing on the next quarter's numbers. Not much enthusiasm, no excitement. In fact, the only emotion in the equation is when we miss the numbers. Then I get upset."

"Let's look at this from another angle," said Jason. "You mentioned the wolf pack earlier. Have you had an opportunity to get a close look at what's going on there?"

"Well, it's difficult to avoid those crazy wolves—they're everywhere. And Mark's reports over the last month have been exceptional. But I can't say I really have a grasp on how he's doing what he's doing. I do know his team is motivated and on task, and they seem to really be enjoying themselves. Now that you mention it, it does remind me of the early days."

"There's a lot of spirit there," said Jason.

"So maybe PRIMETEC could rate a five on the spirit scale after all," said Leon.

Jason nodded assent. "I'd say there's spirit growing in parts of the company. You just haven't been noticing it for what it is. It's like Mark has planted some seeds, he's watering them, and you've been looking the other way to a certain extent. And that's pretty understandable. As the CEO of a growing company, you've put your focus almost exclusively on the numbers, haven't you?"

"Well, yes," said Leon. "It seems essential with the high stakes we're up against, so much pressure to perform in the short term. I just don't have time for the wolf pack thing."

Jason's face grew dead serious. "At the risk of being too forward," he said, "I invite you to consider the possibility that you can't afford not to have time. It's easy to fall into the habit of overlooking spirit, but in the early days you made time without even thinking about it, isn't that right?"

Leon nodded, and Jason continued, "It's possible the conflict you're in right now may be a direct result of not paying attention to such things."

"That's what Helen kept trying to tell me," said Leon. "You're saying I should have listened."

"From what you've told me, and from what I've seen, Helen is an example of the new leadership that is required for success today. People with her skills and sensibilities are emerging in companies to enhance power and effectiveness by helping to heal organizations from the inside, among other things. But they can only thrive if their environments support them. The first prerequisite for a supportive environment is a person at the top with those same qualities, the qualities of a healer. People are hurting in the aftermath of all the change that's come down—downsizing, mergers and acquisitions, reengineering everything in sight. Command and control is bankrupted as a leadership style. It's torn the heart out of business."

"So, you're saying I need to become a healer." The challenge registered on Leon's face—gravity laced with dismay.

"Not exactly," said Jason. "I'll go a step further and say that you already are one in a way. Let me explain. The shamanic tradition says there is a healer in each of us. It's like somewhere tucked away in our genetic encoding there is the memory of a healer in the bloodline, in our cellular memory. If you go back far enough in your genealogy, sooner or later you'll find a healer. Does that make any sense to you?"

"I'm not sure," said Leon. "I think you're telling me I could actually be something I've never thought of being. It hasn't even crossed my mind. Why would I want to do that? Besides, isn't that your job?"

"It's the job of every leader who truly deserves the title," said Jason.

"I'm trying to follow you here," said Leon, "but I don't understand what you're asking of me. Am I going to be dispensing herbs and holding hands at bedside?"

Jason laughed. "Not at all. Here's what I mean specifically. The first tool of a healer is compassion. The second is strength. As the top leader of your organization, it's your job to use those two qualities in a safe, consistent way to help bring balance into the work environment. Then you'll see magic start to happen.

"But the balancing act only begins there. There are many polarities that must be balanced to maximize human productivity and ingenuity. The leader must constantly manage the paradox of opposites like technology and the human element; telling people what to do and empowering them to think for themselves; being tough and being compassionate; focusing on short-term objectives and fostering long-term sustainability. One of the toughest polarities for power people is knowing that sometimes you'll have solutions and sometimes you won't. It means you have to let go of your ego and accept on occasion that you just don't know . . . and what's more, be willing to admit it."

Leon was both fascinated and put off. There's a polarity right there, he thought to himself. "I don't want to become a bleeding heart," he said, voicing one extreme.

"Balance is about being both the healer and the warrior," said Jason. "Remember? Compassion and strength. It's essential that you have both. It's just that the warrior gets a lot more training and support in our current system than the healer."

"So," said Leon, coming around, "somewhere in my ancestry there is a healer and I carry that memory in my DNA. Is that what you said?"

"Yes, and the process I mentioned earlier can help you discover the healer in you," said Jason. "It's a closed-eye journey . . . to meet your ancestral healer. Your healer within."

Jason's words were way too "soft" for King's comfort zone. They set the cells in his body to dancing. Half danced with fear like the choking man in the dream. Half danced with excitement at the promise of a new kind of power, like the horned "Sorcerer of Les Trois Frères."

ELEVEN

In the upper world, they gather, warming spirits by the fire. A host of ancient healers, shamans waiting to be called. Old, closed passageways have opened; new seekers find their way. Bright, wet paints are drawn across new masks and shamans' tools. Fresh hides are fashioned into robes, lovingly sewn. Rocks are ground to powder, slowing time and shaping minds. A crown no longer serves the king. He places it to rest and sets instead upon his head the shaman's feathered crest.

Those who have walked the path of personal transformation will tell you it's a journey not to be taken lightly, but an adventure of the first magnitude, both magically consuming and profoundly challenging. For Leon King, Jason Hand's invitation to journey to his ancestral healer that Monday morning was the gateway to such an adventure. Like most people pausing at an important threshold, he sensed there would be no going back—that opting for a seemingly simple exploration of his internal terrain could be the choice of a lifetime.

The magnitude of the moment had nothing to do with the shamanic journey itself. That was just the vehicle. His gateway could have been one of any number of things intersecting his life at just the right moment. A shamanic journey is like most processes—its dimensions are directly tied to the circumstances in which it takes place. For Mark Steed it had been a relatively impersonal quest, journeying to retrieve a power animal for the group. And for Leon King, the journey would be a powerful personal experience, and he sensed as much.

He couldn't sit still as he waited for Jason to return from a rest-room break. He paced the room, glancing at the many unusual objects and artifacts around him. They only served to emphasize his feeling of being in alien territory. I'm not sure about this, he thought. Am I going to make a fool of myself here? He was aware as he asked it that his question was a guise, a cover for bigger feelings that lay just below his surface. He didn't want to admit it even to himself, but he was scared.

He replayed his conversation with Jason, looking for reassurance. Jason had answered enough questions to satisfy his logical mind, and his intuition was telling him he could benefit by taking a chance here. But his emotions were still at odds—trepidation and anticipation tugging at him by turns. He felt he'd come too far to back out. To beg off, he'd have to make a lame excuse to Jason, and he had the feeling the man would see right through him. No, he had set his course, and he would follow through. This final decision was prompted by a truth that was central to his life experience; challenges well met are the juice of life. He would not shy from this one, however strange or awkward he might feel as he immersed himself in it.

Jason dimmed the lights in the room as he entered, then pulled his chair up to his exotically decorated drum. "So," he said, "are you ready to give this a try?"

"Sure," said Leon, his words just one breath behind his decision. "Let's do it."

As he had done with Mark, Jason began by giving Leon an orientation to shamanic journeying. His intention would be to meet his ancestral healer. For that he would journey to the upper world. It was a nonordinary state of consciousness, a place where he could get help without interference from his logical mind. He would lie down with a blindfold over his eyes while Jason drummed.

"What's the drumming for?" asked Leon.

"You know how in the movies you always see a witch doctor or medicine man with a drum or a rattle?" said Jason. "Well, that's because the repetitive sound of those instruments facilitates a change in consciousness. Technically, they induce an alpha or theta state. Shamans say the sonic drive of a drum or a rattle has the same vibration as the earth. It's why we give rattles to babies when we want them to go to sleep. The soft monotonous sound relaxes them."

"Is it like hypnotism? I mean, I'm not going to find myself suddenly scratching my ear uncontrollably tomorrow, or something like that, because you've given me a posthypnotic suggestion, am I?"

Jason smiled. "Not at all. You have complete control of the journey. I just help you get into a state of mind that allows you to access your own realm of possibilities. Let me give you an example. Have you ever driven from the city out to your home and realized once you got there that you couldn't remember the drive at all?"

"Sure," said Leon. "Sometimes it makes me wonder where my mind went."

"Well, it probably went into an alpha state. Sometimes we

go there automatically when we need a rest or a different perspective. We can function perfectly, but most of our mind is somewhere else. Does that answer your question?"

Leon nodded and listened intently as Jason continued to prepare him for the journey. Once the basic orientation was complete, Jason said, "Just let the drumbeats carry you through whatever passage you've chosen to enter the upper world. Once you're there, trust whatever you see. You'll be looking for your ancestral healer. It may or may not make itself known to you. If it does, you can check that it is your ancestral healer. Just ask him . . . or her. Then trust. The less you question what you're experiencing, the more impact it will have for you."

"You're asking me to go pretty far out on a limb," said Leon, aware of his anxiety rising again. "Do you ever run into somebody who just can't do this?"

"Sometimes people find their first journey to be difficult, but with time they're usually able to do it," said Jason. "Bottom line is, if you don't experience anything, that's okay. This isn't about performance. It's about possibility. If it doesn't work for you this time, trust that it was not meant to be. But I would encourage you to expect surprises. My experience is that spirit will give you just what you need. The greatest challenge is more likely to be setting questions aside and trusting what you see."

"Okay," said Leon, thinking to himself, I guess I wouldn't be here this morning if I weren't ready to give this a try.

Jason picked up on his thoughts. "I appreciate your sense of adventure," he said. "And your questions aren't unusual. You're going into uncharted territory here, and it does require that you make a leap of faith."

Jason's eyes probed like lasers, discerning whether Leon was really ready to proceed. "It may sound far-fetched," he said, "but there are no limitations in the upper and lower worlds—they are not bound by time and space. You could fly around or even walk through a tree. Sometimes there are all kinds of things going on, lots of action."

It might have been nervous tension or even the need for a small measure of control, but Leon leaned over and thumped the drum sharply. "Isn't that pretty loud?" he asked. "I sure as heck don't want anybody coming in here to check out the noise."

"It's okay," Jason assured him. "These walls are pretty thick, and we're the only ones within earshot. Ready?"

Jason reminded Leon that just prior to journeying to the upper world he should restate his intention to find his ancestral healer. Leon settled back, putting the blindfold over his eyes and breathing deeply as he'd been coached to do. He had chosen as his entrance an old chimney amid the rubble of a burned house he used to play near as a kid. The drumming began, and after a few seconds, in his mind's eye, he plunged inside the chimney entrance, into the dark, enchanted by the feeling that engulfed him, a feeling of floating high into the sky as though attached to a giant invisible balloon.

He was surfing a moment of wonder, then magically floating up and up through endless shades of soft pastel. Color shifted to form, and what had been a pale green blur became a stand of trees, thickening and darkening in contrast to the azure air. I'm looking for my ancestral healer, he thought, prompting himself, as he realized he was standing on solid ground in the deep woods.

He heard the sound of voices and headed off through the brush to investigate. Darkness settled in almost like dusk as he made his way beneath a thick umbrella of pine boughs. In the distance he saw the blaze of a bonfire and the shadows of people standing in a circle around it. One figure stood taller than the rest. As Leon cautiously approached, he saw the man wore a luxurious robe of finely tanned reindeer hide that draped to his ankles, an artful rendering of the animal itself across the back. Towering up was a headdress of noble plumes. He guessed by the man's stature that he was a person of some importance, a leader perhaps. He wondered how it might feel to join that circle.

No sooner was the thought formed than the man turned. He held in his hand a staff with strips of hide, fur, and feathers wrapped around intricate carvings. He waved it gracefully, inviting Leon to join them.

Up close, the man's face was a living maze of deep lines that promised without question that every expression known to mankind had a comfortable home there. The pupils of his eyes opened onto eternity, tiny pinpoints of light forming constellations in some timeless night sky. He gazed at Leon intently for a moment and said in a deep, full voice, "Why are you here?"

He was so direct, so serious, and yet so personal that Leon was caught off guard, thinking to himself, this seems so real. His answer sprang forth unplanned from deep in his own shadow lands: "To rediscover my healer within."

He reeled as the clarity of his own truth registered in his mind. He was more than a little surprised and just a bit proud of himself as well, assuming in the cracks of the moment that he had surely just said something quite splendid. But the man looked at him without expression and said, "Why?"

Again, Leon lost his place. His ability to look inside for answers was being tested. It prompted him to dig deeper and say, "Because I've lost my way as a leader. And being out of touch has hurt my company. And more important, it's hurt people who are very dear to me." He couldn't believe what he was saying; his words were prying his thoughts open more and more, letting the light of truth shine in on long-hidden secrets.

"If I help you find this part, what will you do with it?" said the man. He spoke in a strong accent, Celtic or German perhaps.

"I don't know," said Leon. "I just know I feel incomplete and I can't be the leader I want to be." He was way out on a limb. He needed some grounding. His mind turned to logic, and he thought to ask, "Are you my ancestral healer?"

The man's eyes twinkled ever so slightly as he solemnly said, "Yes."

If there had been a "wow" in Leon King's vocabulary, it would have voiced itself in that moment. He felt proud that he was in some way connected to this impressive, wise being. His sense of awe posed another question in his mind. "What is your name?" he asked.

From lost ages the answer came in thick brogue: "Eolas."

The striking man began walking slowly toward him. Time and space dissolved, and the music of the spheres played tribute to the moment. Leon's body—his whole being—expanded as though to make room for more strands of DNA, three, four, five . . . The man moved closer and closer, his body fading ever so slightly with each step until at last Leon was alone, but he had the feeling he'd never been in better company. His chest expanded, breathing in a sense a peace and comfort. An object filled his hand—the ornately carved fur-bound staff—and suddenly Leon knew exactly what to do. He examined the staff very carefully, etching it into his memory, a design to be crafted one day into a real object, in the three-dimensional world.

The journey was complete, there was no question of that, and Leon began retracing his steps to return to normal consciousness. He left behind the circle of night figures and found his way back through the forest, which reversed itself as he went into shades of pink and yellow, blue and green. He floated down into the chimney and back to the couch in Jason's office.

While his mind caught up with him, Leon listened to the final beats of the drum, then seconds of silence. He took the blindfold off and blinked open his eyes, thankful for the subtle lighting in the room.

Jason asked, "How do you feel?"

"I haven't felt this peaceful in months," he said. "Maybe years."

"Did you find your ancestral healer?"

"Yes," Leon said, a combination of wonder and shyness in his voice. "He was an amazing character." The words weren't adequate to the task. "He left a staff in my hand, an exotic carved thing with feathers and fur hanging from it. I'm pretty sure he wanted me to make one like it sometime."

"It's his way of staying with you," said Jason. "He'll always be there now, as a resource, a constant source of healing energy. You can make him even more welcomed in your world by calling his name. Do you know what it is?"

As though he had said it all his life, the name rolled off Leon's tongue: "Eolas." A blush washed over him as he realized the extent to which, in just a short time, he'd gotten comfortable with the shaman ways. "I didn't know what to expect," he said, "and I'm not sure I do now. I just know something remarkable has happened." His eyes met Jason's. "Thank you."

It was done, and the real world tugged at Leon. He had so many things to do, but as he finished up with Jason and made his way back to his office, he felt a lightness and renewed confidence. There was a lot of ground to cover. He would repair things with John and Helen, and though he didn't know exactly how, he trusted that he had, within himself, a new source of power—power honed by wisdom.

He spread the blue memo sheets out again across his desk. John, Helen, Mark, Maria, Frank . . . he could almost feel them breathing. He smiled at Mark with kinship and a new level of respect. Maria . . . she's been doing so great, he thought to himself almost like a father whose daughter was at the top of her class. Helen . . . I miss her. I've got to find a way to get her to the meeting tomorrow. John . . . he could see his face, happy-go-lucky, a real kid spirit and a solid team player. I've got to find him right now, he thought. But before he picked up the phone to begin his search, he stared at the one remaining name, Frank. A grim realization overtook him.

I've got to let him go, he thought. There's no question. When all this is played out, he'll have lost the respect of the others, and his need for power is too great. He'll never be appropriate to a healthy environment here.

Then, as often happens when one realizes that an ancient piece of personal history must be plucked out, Leon felt a compassionate sadness possess him. He really does try, he thought. We've been together for so many years. We built PRIMETEC from the ground up. Firing Frank will leave a hole that will gape for a long time to come. I'll find a way to tell him first thing in the morning.

Tracking John down was no easy chore. Leon called at least a dozen times that morning. He was determined to apologize and make sure John would come in to attend the meeting he'd scheduled for Tuesday. At noon, he gave up calling and ordered a limo to take him across the river to John's home. He was more than a little nervous about facing the man after all that had happened. As they drove through the Lincoln Tunnel, he thought about Eolas, wondering just how he would make himself known here in the real world.

His answer came the moment he saw the stricken look on John's face when his front door opened. Leon was consumed by a wave of compassion and deep regret. He looked John directly in the eye, extended his hand, and said, "I'm here to say I'm so sorry for the mess I got you into over the weekend. You're very important to me and to PRIMETEC. Can we talk?"

Over the ensuing hour, Leon told John the whole story of what had happened on Friday. He was careful to keep the responsibility in his own charge, referring to Frank only as was absolutely necessary to convey the truth. "It was entirely my fault," he said. "I let things slip and gave Frank too much latitude, but I want you to know that I never for a moment intended to put you out of PRIMETEC. You're an important asset and I need you. We need you."

The conversation never really warmed, but when it was over, both men agreed they would do what they could to start again. John would come back into the office on Tuesday, and Leon would work to make him glad he had.

The Tuesday meeting was scheduled for ten. As he prepared that morning, Leon's stomach churned. He was still recovering from the load of anger he'd gotten from Frank earlier. He'd lashed out with bitter venom as if he'd hated Leon for years, and he raved about making trouble in the press. "I've done it before, and I'll do it again," Frank had said. I'll check it out later, Leon thought as he tried to shake the weight of the encounter, but the threat had only served to reinforce his decision to let Frank go.

Now he needed to get his head straight for the meeting with his team. He would take a completely different approach this morning, no planned speeches, no edicts, no . . . well, in truth, he didn't have any idea what he was going to say. He leaned back in his chair and closed his eyes. He could see Eolas's face in his imagination. I wonder what he'd tell me, he thought to himself. Clear as a bell, the rich voice sounded in Leon's ears: "Speak from your heart. No notes, no agendas. Keep it short and real . . . and listen."

Helen Singer was dressed to the nines that Tuesday morning as she came into the building. She held her head high and made her way to Maria's office. "I'm sorry I upset you on Friday," she said as she reached for a hug.

"Well, you don't look like you're too upset now," said Maria. "What's up? What are you going to do?"

"I've made up my mind," she said, "but I want to save the details for the meeting. You know, say it one time and make sure everybody gets the same story." They both laughed knowingly. It had taken several phone conversations on Monday for them both to unwind their contributions to the tangled PRIMETEC mess, and they were still a little sheepish.

In contrast, John Conatello was pretty guarded as he made his way to the boardroom. He wanted to believe all the things Leon had said to him the day before, but he wasn't sure he could trust him anymore. He had stopped by Maria's office, too, and apologized for hanging up on her. She was thrilled to see him back on the job. "I was mortified when I realized you were hearing that awful news for the first time from me," she said. "I'm so glad it turned out not to be true, but I still feel pretty silly."

TWELVE

Shaman climbs to mountaintops and treads through steep city canyons. He travels alone, has for ages, heeding cries of pain, crying tears of peace, set apart by a gentle heart from family, friends, and tribe. No politics command him, no price purchases his favor.

Reaching across the ages, he touches the many skins of humankind, red, white, and black, yellow and brown. He digs down into the pulsing open heart of them, where all color is the same pink flesh, and pulls out the dark plagues. He helps the old skins loosen and fall away when their time has come. He soothes and heals and nurtures the new. And then, as magically as he came, he goes his shaman's way.

Helen purposely sat in the same chair she had occupied at the fateful meeting in August. She chose it as a grounding point for her perceptions. She'd been deeply moved by a visit from Leon the night before, but wondered if the change she'd seen in him would carry forward into the meeting today and into the future beyond. The boardroom and her accustomed seat in it would serve as mirrors, highlighting his true colors in her view. As she waited, her mind drifted back to the day before.

It was about two-thirty Monday afternoon when Leon first called from the limo on his way back from New Jersey. He asked if he could come by for a few minutes. Helen had felt pressured, not at all inclined to face him, but she knew that sooner or later she would have to. Not wanting her privacy invaded, she suggested the deli on the corner as a place to meet.

She arrived nervous, tentative, secretly hoping he would come through in some unpredictably wonderful way and wipe the whole mess clean. She took a table by the window and watched, eager to gauge his mood as he arrived.

In the spaces of his day, Leon had continued to search for a way to approach Helen. He was relieved by his meeting with John, but it left him with a sense of urgency—as if he still had an unavoidable item to check off his "to do" list. A dozen strategies pulled at him. It wouldn't be enough simply to apologize, making promises would only put her off, and it would be fruitless to try reason with so much emotion in play. He needed something with more power to it.

Then he had it. The limo darted into a loading zone and he got out confident in his ability to confront the situation openly and bring Helen home to PRIMETEC.

The deli was quiet, just a few late lunchers finishing up and a takeout order. Without a moment's hesitation, Leon sat down across from Helen and said, "We just have to get through this. I've messed up, but it doesn't have to end like this." To himself he was thinking, Remember to be a healer, but his mind was racing, urging him into the only action that made sense right then. "I want to heal the rift between us," he said, "and I'm prepared to make you an offer you can't refuse. PRIMETEC needs a strong president. Tell me what you want in the way of salary and the position's yours."

The power of his words overwhelmed Helen. Her head cocked back, palms flat against the table. Years of career planning flashed before her . . . president of the company . . . the offer of a lifetime. But a sick, dark feeling oozed through her and her pupils contracted, focusing inward. I should jump at this, she thought, he's saying the right words . . . but it's all wrong. . . . I should be honored, but I feel dirty, sleazy. Then the light dawned: he wanted her back on a bribe.

So much for fairy tales, she thought, sliding her chair back. As she rose, her exit line seethed audible steam: "You just don't get it, do you?" And she was gone.

Leon's next word scorched the deli walls and rebounded as burning fact: I blew it—some ancient healer I am! Feeling more like a clumsy dinosaur, he slumped into the limo. He was frustrated, and his first thought was to curse the whole shaman thing, but he was too powerfully affected by his time with Jason to write it off at the first sign of a problem. He soon realized that his approach with Helen was far from what Jason would have advised. I'd better get a refresher course, he admitted to himself, and he dialed PRIMETEC reception, having forgotten to get the shaman's direct number earlier.

By the time he reached Jason's space, Leon was deep in anguished self-reflection. Helen was right; he didn't get it. The quiet self-assurance he'd felt earlier in his meeting with John was gone. Everything had seemed so clear then, his every move a right step. Now he was drowning in a pool of good intentions. "What am I missing?" he asked Jason after a brief synopsis of his two very different encounters.

The quiet strength of Jason's demeanor was reassuring as Leon sat poised to listen. "You're not missing anything," the shaman said. "You just slipped a little. It's to be expected. You're rewiring a lifetime of habitual behavior. There's no way you're going to change all at once. And this is very subtle stuff."

Jason surveyed the energy in the room and found it wanting. He reached for his sage stick and a match. "Let's start by clearing the air a bit," he said, lighting the bundled herb. "This is called smudging. It's a method native peoples use to remove negative energy." Aromatic smoke wafted through the room. Leon didn't know why, but he felt comforted by the smoke of the sage and the movement of Jason's hand as he waved it gently about, saying matter-of-factly, "Let's just invite any unhelpful spirits to leave the room."

When the smudging was done and both men were seated, Jason continued, "Maybe it would help to look at what did work for you today."

"Well, as I said, I did a pretty good job of starting new with John. At least he's willing to come back in and give me a chance. He didn't exactly embrace me with open arms, but we did reach a sort of gentlemen's agreement. Should I have pushed for more?"

"It sounds like you were very appropriate with John," said Jason, "showing him genuine respect and taking the first step to reestablish trust. His remaining resistance is natural. There's a lot of history between you two, and you're asking him to set that aside and see that you've truly changed."

"But the change is in John's favor," said Leon. "Doesn't he know that?"

"The more important the change is to John and the more he might want it, the harder it will be for him to accept it. He's suffered a loss of faith, and he's not likely to set himself up for another one. This is a very delicate time between you. Your change, no matter how welcomed, has the effect of making you unpredictable to John. He's used to relying on you to be a certain way. It may take months for him to believe that your new behavior is for real. Did you tell him directly that you were committed to changing your approach at PRIMETEC?"

"Not really."

"Well, I suggest you do so when you have the opportunity. The more direct you can be about what you're trying to do, the more support you can expect from others. And you'll find that clearly stating what you're doing will also commit you more deeply yourself."

"I see what you mean. This really is a pretty big deal, isn't it?" said Leon.

"Yes, it is," said Jason. "One of the biggest adjustments you'll have to make is getting used to asking for support. Changing core behavior is always challenging. That's why ninety-eight percent of the people who go on a diet fail to keep the weight off. They need more than their own resolve to stay on track, and you'll need the support of others to sustain this change in your behavior at PRIMETEC. If you have some trusted allies, you'd do well to ask for their assistance—let them coach you and invite them to let you know when you're getting off track."

"Oh, great," said Leon. "My most trusted ally wants my head in a basket right now. I just never realized how important Helen's support was. How am I going to solve that one?"

Jason answered with a question: "What's your assessment of your behavior with her this afternoon?"

"It was a power play," said Leon. "A stupid reversion to my old command and control. I could kick myself."

It was a pivotal moment, and Jason gave it space before he

responded thoughtfully, "This journey will not be easy. It's likely that for some time you will be tempted to slip into old methods. You'll have to trust that there is a new part of you emerging and help it come forth as best you can. When you do slip, have compassion for yourself, correct the error, learn from it, and move on."

"Why did I slip today, though? I was doing so well."

"Usually there's a pattern involved, a setup of some kind. How were you feeling when you made your decision to offer Helen the promotion?"

Leon closed his eyes and recalled his limo ride, "After being with John I was fine, but by the time I got back into the city, I was feeling the intense pressure of having to get Helen back into the fold. I shifted to automatic, just going through the moves, trying to get the job done . . . and I see now that I used my power as CEO to address the problem instead of my inner healer. I was telling myself I wanted a healing to happen, but I didn't make any space for it."

"So, what you can learn from this," said Jason, "is that it's counterproductive for you to make important decisions when you've got a closed agenda or when you feel pressured. Those are triggers for you, preludes to self-sabotage and blocks to creating a win."

Leon was pensive. "I really thought the presidency would be a win for Helen."

"It wasn't necessarily the promotion that was wrong, it was the circumstances surrounding it and the way you delivered it. A change like that would be significant for Helen. My guess is that she would have liked it to come at a time when things were working well between you, when she trusted you to be a partner in helping her make the best decision. Right now, her faith in you is shattered, so it's likely she felt caught in your desperate ambush."

"You're right," said Leon, "I started out sincerely concerned about Helen's welfare, but by the time I got to her, I was dead set on having my way. And I pulled out the ace I thought would manipulate her into responding the way I wanted her to."

"Good, that's very good," said Jason. "What else can you see here?"

"A healing approach would have required me to stay open to whatever outcome would support both of us," said Leon. "A win-win. I would need to engage her in the process somehow. But how? I mean, how can I even dare call her now that I've dug myself deeper into this hole?"

"Show your respect for Helen in your actions as you did with John today. Give her all the latitude she needs to say no to you right now, or vent her anger. Then trust the right thing will happen. You have Eolas to guide you. Keep constant council with him, and when you feel the time is right, ask for his wisdom." Jason looked directly into Leon's eyes. "You'll do fine," he said.

Though she hadn't been privy to this conversation between Jason and Leon, Helen had certainly felt the effects of it that evening when Leon called from his car asking once again if they could talk. The warmth and genuine humility in his voice was marked, even over the phone. Curiosity tugged at her guard until it fell, helped by the fact that she'd just come from the gym, where she'd punched a bag for forty-five minutes saying "Leon King" repeatedly under her breath. Her energy was strong and clear and she felt she could hold her own with him and not lose her temper. She agreed to a walk, thinking that the freedom of the open air would be an ally to her. Once on the street, she set a lively pace, still feeling the burn of her muscles from the gym.

The two of them didn't say a word for several blocks, the tenseness between them a formidable wall. They walked briskly, with Leon keeping pace a step or two behind, their footfalls tapping out a steady cadence. The movement, the fresh air, and the rhythm as they walked had the effect of relaxing his mind even further, until it slid into a plain and simple question: What should I do?

"Just tell her your truth as it exists in this moment," came the answer in Eolas's resonant tone. It stopped Leon in his tracks. He closed his eyes to catch a glimpse of the wise one, and muttered, "Thank you," recognizing as he spoke that the only way to reach through Helen's resistance was to take her into his confidence, way in.

When he opened his eyes, they were bright with moisture. "There's no reason why you should believe what I'm about to tell you," he said. "I'm not sure how I came to believe it myself, but I have a story I'd like very much for you to hear."

Helen looked at him as though he were an apparition. She had seen him a thousand times in her mind's eye just as he stood there now, composed, peaceful, and in command—not necessarily of the situation—but of himself. It had been her dream for him, that he could one day step into his power with full authenticity, and in that moment he was doing so. It was undeniable in the character of his stance—the power that comes from vulnerability. This was a man she could respect. If he wanted her attention, he would have it.

"Why don't we get a glass of wine," she said. "There's a place on sixty-eighth street." They walked a block and a half, chose a sidewalk table, and ordered two glasses of merlot. Then Leon told his story.

He began by describing his interaction with Frank on Friday morning, admitting that he had abdicated responsibility. He told about his sail and the disturbing phone call from Frank. "When I heard you had threatened to quit, I got blazing mad and blamed Frank. But this morning when I found your resignation letter on my desk, I realized it was all tied to my own lapse in judgment."

Leon lowered his eyes to follow his fingers around the rim of his glass, then looked up and said, "It made me realize how much I've been depending on you these past months. I know it hasn't seemed like it to you because of the distance I've kept, but I see now that I was counting on you to do the right thing, even when I didn't."

He described the remorse that had welled up in him as he sailed north on Saturday and the nasty nightmare that had waked him Sunday morning. Helen sat transfixed by the strange vision of Leon hanging from a tree, choking himself, his feet dancing, with Frank wrestling the snake down below. "The most amazing part, though," he said, "was this traveler who stopped to ask me why I was choking myself. I'd never seen the guy before, but darned if I didn't run into him at the coffee station first thing this morning. You know who it turned out to be? Jason Hand, the person Maria brought in to consult in marketing. I couldn't believe it!" He was very animated now, expressing and describing with the wonderment of a child. "There he was big as life making tea . . . and that's just the beginning of that story."

Helen knew she was listening to a very different Leon King. He had been places she never would have guessed he

would venture, and he had seen those places through remark-
ably new eyes. He backtracked and told how shocked he'd been
when Maria called to tell him about John. "It felt like the end
of the world—first you, then John. I'd been hoping he would
never have to know." As he talked, he seemed to be assembling
all the pieces of the story for the first time. "I knew I needed to
take action, but I didn't know how until I talked to Mark."

Leon stared off into the urban night, but he didn't see the
lights, or the traffic, or the people going by. He saw only the
extraordinary adventure he had taken in Jason Hand's office.
He reined his attention in again and talked about it, his voice
round and rich. Helen traced every inflection. She couldn't
believe what she was hearing, but she knew in her heart it was
all true . . . the drumming, the journey, the circle of night figures, the shaman healer, the staff, all of it. And she felt she was
witnessing miracles . . . for herself, the possibility of finding a
renewed sense of belonging at PRIMETEC, and for her friend
Leon King, the possibility that he had truly found new meaning in the word "leadership." This was affirmed as Leon asked
her about her feelings that resulted from recent events, particularly the bungled job offer. She noted that he listened
empathically with no apparent defensiveness.

Helen brought her attention back to the boardroom as the
other members of the executive committee gathered. They
were puzzled by the bare table—no financial reports. Mark
and Maria assumed that Frank had been detained and would
be there to pass them out soon. John was hoping against hope
that Frank Farratt would never walk through the big
mahogany doors again.

Leon arrived exactly on time, oddly unencumbered, no files

or folders, not even a notepad in his hand. "We're going to break with convention this morning," he said. "This will be a short meeting and a rather informal one. I need to fill you in on some things that have happened over the past five days, and I want to begin by apologizing to you, each of you.

"I'm afraid I've made some big mistakes recently, and as a result, some of you have suffered quite a bit. Before I do that, I want to explain Frank's absence this morning." Leon's voice cracked painfully. "I spoke with him a bit ago to let him know he would be leaving the company. I won't go into the details behind my decision, but I will say that on the surface it was the result of inappropriate independent actions he had taken. With that said, let me clarify that I had collusion in those actions. I wasn't minding the store closely enough. I've known Frank for a long time, and I like to think he was doing what he truly believed he needed to do for PRIMETEC."

He was shaken as he finished his statement, almost in tears. He took a moment to compose himself, then began his apologies with a warmth in his voice none in the room, save Helen, had heard before. "John, you took a big hit over the weekend because I dropped the ball on important issues. I hope you can forgive me. I don't have any excuses. I lost my grip on what was going on around here. I will do everything I can to make it up to you, and I'll start by putting those darned receivables back where they belong, in the accounting department. It's not appropriate for your people to carry the added weight of collections when they're grinding so hard for sales. The truth is, we're going to miss our numbers again this quarter, but I'm holding myself responsible. If you're in danger of missing a target, let me know what I can do. I'll be happy to help.

"Maria, you got caught in the middle of the mess with

John. You reached out to give support and ended up inadvertently setting off a bomb. I'm truly sorry about that. The fault lies with me. Please forgive me for the embarrassment I've caused you.

"Helen, yesterday you left your resignation on my desk. I believe you were entirely justified in doing so under the circumstances you encountered on Friday, and I'm terribly sorry for having put you in that position. I know you've come here today with an open mind. Thank you for that. Your value to the company has never been higher. We need you here to help make some changes . . . big changes. There'll be a meeting tomorrow to start the process. I'm glad you have chosen to attend.

"Mark, you're probably wondering what all this is about. I'm sure the rumor mill has filled you in on some of what's happened, and I'll answer any questions you have after we're through here, but I want you to know that you really helped me out yesterday when you backed the idea that I should talk with Jason Hand. I met with him yesterday, and I'd like to share with you, all of you, a little of the remarkable things I learned."

Leon's new, more vulnerable self was clearly speaking now. He hadn't slowed down enough in his delivery to listen as much as Eolas had advised him to do, but what he was about to say would be enough to demonstrate to everyone in the room that they had a new CEO. He was visibly grasping for the right words.

"When a company doesn't do well, you've got to look at the leader. PRIMETEC is in trouble, and I've come to realize that the problem is me." There was no self-reproach in his tone, only the pristine ring of truth. "I've been putting a lot of pressure on all of you, asking for the moon. But I haven't done my part to get you the support you need. On the contrary, I've been making things hard for you, expecting you to work in a vacuum to solve problems that affect us all. I've let myself be run by the numbers, and I forgot for a while that it takes good people to get good numbers. What I know now is that it takes a good leader to keep good people. I don't know how good a leader I can be, but I know there are a lot of things I can try, and I'm telling you right now, I'll do whatever I can to create the kind of environment where we can all flourish.

"We have some serious repair work to do. It's come to my attention that some of our reports over the past year have been inaccurate. That includes our current figures. We're in a worse position than we thought. Our projections this quarter were overly ambitious. We've got to back off and regroup, and more important, we've got to work together. I'll take the heat from Wall Street—that was my gamble—and you can count on me to get you whatever help you need to prepare your departments for success over the next year."

In those few moments, Leon King stepped to the front line and joined his troops in the field. He came though not just as their general, but as their healer as well, a kind of compassionate medic, and through his dedication and force of will over the years to come, he would transform the role to noble heights. He never went back on his word, and PRIMETEC became a far more successful company than any had dreamed it could be. It didn't come easily—it never does. The wheels of a big company turn slowly, adjusting layer by layer as new ideas are introduced. Reluctance must be overcome, trials must be run. Priorities must be set and constantly reviewed. Early successes must be celebrated and built upon, but these are the tasks of renewal, and renewal is the heart of healing. It can only take place when the old, dead skin is shed and new life is set free.

The meeting was just breaking up when Jason Hand stuck his head in the door to say goodbye. He shook hands all around. Then he turned to Maria with a big smile and a squeeze of her shoulders. She had been the link. It was Maria's willingness to look beyond the surface that had opened each subsequent door for herself and PRIMETEC. He knew she would thrive as he watched her move confidently among her peers, no longer that frightened little girl in the shadow of a fearsome father.

Jason turned and headed off to say his last goodbye to Leon. The two men shook hands and silently acknowledged the work they had done together. Jason was confident that Leon had the perspective and power he needed to heal his company and his people. He watched with pride as Leon moved back into the circle of his leadership team, the men and women upon whom he depended for the very being of his company.

Experience told the shaman his work was done. He recognized the sound of excitement underscored with positive intent, the banter of the wolf pack making its way through rough terrain. He smiled and turned to leave, pulling his overcoat loosely around his shoulders. No one noticed as it spread a vibrant spectrum across the boardroom door just before its heavy brass latch came home to rest.

ADDENDUM

Are You Ready for Your Own Shamanic Journey?

I hope you enjoyed *The Corporate Shaman*. This section has been added for those of you who would like to explore shamanism and, in particular, the shamanic journey a little more. For many readers the book raises issues that are both work-related and personal. The questions below are designed to augment and deepen whatever insights you have gained from reading *The Corporate Shaman* and, if you choose, to prepare you to take your own shamanic journey. I hope you find them useful.

For everyone:
1. What insights have you gained in reading *The Corporate Shaman*? About yourself? About the organization in which you work?
2. If and when you feel dispirited at work, what is the cause?
3. If and when your organization's spirit flounders, what is the cause?
4. What can you do to build spirit in your organization?
5. What can you do to enrich your work life?
6. Have you ever tried looking for meaningful symbols in the world around you to guide and enrich your daily experience of

life? If not, is this something you believe would benefit you?

7. What feelings arise when you think about taking a shamanic journey?

8. To what extent do you trust and act on your intuition?

9. To whom do you turn when you feel dispirited or demotivated?

For leaders and managers:

1. To whom do you confide when you feel dispirited or demotivated?

2. To what extent do you use and trust your intuition in making important decisions?

3. What reflections and insights do you have about your own leadership style?

4. To what extent are you willing to step outside your normal way of doing things and try an alternative approach?

5. How much consideration do you give to the impact your decisions will have on the people who will be affected by them?

6. How would you rate yourself on your willingness to be candid with other people?

7. To what extent are you able to be vulnerable in work situations as opposed to always having to have the "right" answer?

8. To what extent are you willing to drop your own agenda and truly seek out and listen to others' points of view?

9. To what extent are you able to be with others when they are emotional and not think less of them or try to fix the problem?

I would be very interested in your reactions to *The Corporate Shaman*. What did you like? Not like? How has it affected you? How would you describe it to others? *Have* you recommended it to others? What do you believe are the key messages of the book? Please send your responses to richard@whiteleygroup.com.

How to Take a Shamanic Journey

For most shamans, the shamanic journey is the primary method used to access the other worlds where the spirit helpers are found. While the specific process for journeying may vary from one shaman to another, the steps outlined below are practiced by a great many and are very effective.

You do not have to have any special skills or attributes to conduct a journey. This process is not reserved for a select few "tapped-in" individuals. While some may find journeying challenging, most will be able to master this relatively simple process, if not on the first try, then in a second or third attempt. I remember well my first effort. While a friend drummed the monotonous beat that supports the journey by facilitating a change of one's state of consciousness, I reviewed once again the steps outlined in Michael Harner's classic book *The Way of the Shaman*. I donned my blindfold and successfully entered the lower world for what would be the first of thousands of times.

By journeying to the lower world, as Jason Hand did for Mark, you will be able to find your own power animal and in so doing enrich and empower your life. When found and used, this wonderful animal totem will be your guide and adviser for as long as you wish it to be.

I have found that there are many benefits to journeying. For most people, three stand out. First is that a ten-minute shamanic journey reinvigorates you. You come back refreshed and rested. It is really an easy and most enjoyable form of deep relaxation. I like to call it "meditating for Type A's," because rather than trying to clear your mind of all thoughts as instructed by the meditation teachers, you take a journey so filled with amazing activities that you become a participant in the process and, in so doing, let go the pressures and concerns of your normal day-to-day reality. It is as absorbing as a good movie or engaging book.

The second benefit is that your totem animal will fill you with power. Think of this as being filled with a positive energy that gives you strength to withstand the rigors and stresses of daily life and prevents what shamans call "intrusions" from finding a way into your being. Intrusions are things like disease, depression, chronic bad luck, and the like. Before a challenging meeting with one's boss, for example, or during a white-knuckle flight on an airplane, you can ask your power animal to give you strength and protection.

The third benefit is that your power animal will offer guidance regarding problems or dilemmas you may be facing. This is called divination and means "divining" the answers to important questions. Before I make a speech, for example, I always journey to one of my power animals to learn how I can best serve the audience. And when my son returned from several years working in Chile and was looking for a job, in spite of an excellent job market and a terrific résumé, he had trouble finding a position. After journeying to his power animal he was advised to "just be in your nature." Matthew immediately realized what the advice meant. In his interviews he was trying to be the perfect job candidate . . . to be what they were looking for. As soon as he let that go and showed up as Matthew, he got the offer he wanted.

Although I have never heard of any negative consequence to any individual who has journeyed, if you are uncomfortable with the process, you have several options. (1) Overcome your discomfort. If you don't like the idea of searching for a power animal, ask to find a spirit helper. Or ask yourself, "What's the worst thing that could happen to me if I'm successful?" The answer is usually "Nothing." Ask, "Are there any deep-seated beliefs that make this uncomfortable for me?" Of this, Noelle Poncelet, a clinical psychologist who teaches the shamanic ways in Belgium, France, and Russia, says that some of us carry "beliefs that we are not allowed to journey or practice shamanism for reasons [offered] by specific groups, be it family, religious, or society. Too much freedom? Too much power? Sacrilegious? Power animals are too instinctual, too dangerous, and too base to be spirit helpers. Not my style? Something else? Reexamine that belief. If it still fits your values, then you will know that shamanic journeying is not for you. If not, you will finally be ready to proceed." (2) Ask a shaman practitioner to teach and guide you. (You can find such a trained individual by contacting the Foundation for Shamanic Studies at www.shamanism.org.) (3) Attend one of the foundation's "Introduction to Shamanism" workshops. They are regularly scheduled around the world and will get you journeying in no time at all.

Before the Journey

In order to take such a journey you will need several things:

1. an open mind
2. a clear intention
3. a drumming or rattling tape (These can be bought over the

web at www.shamanism.org. I prefer the multiple drumming tape but any one will work just fine.)
4. a blindfold
5. a quiet place to do the work
6. a mental picture of an entrance to the earth you have seen at some time in your life

Find a quiet and comfortable location where you will not be interrupted. Avoid distractions like telephones ringing, children yelling, and television blaring. When you become proficient at journeying you will be able to do so in your office while sitting at your desk. If a noise or distraction does occur while you are journeying, rather than letting it distract you, simply use it to go deeper into your journey.

Two vital aspects of a successful effort are your starting point and your intention. Your starting point will be an entrance to the earth that is known to you from your own life's experience. A swimming hole, a well, a cave, a tunnel, a hole in the center of an old stump, an uncovered manhole. It should be an entrance the depth or end of which you have not reached. I always use a cave I explored in the Philippines. *It is very important to have a clear image of your place.* You do not have to have entered the entrance, but the picture of it in your mind must be vivid. I find that many people have difficulty when they are learning to journey because they don't have a good departure point.

Once you have your entrance, determine what you want from your journey. Intention is one of the most important and powerful tools used by the shaman. So before each journey, state a single intention for that experience. For your first effort your intention might be "to experience a journey to the lower world to explore." When you have done that, on another journey you might ask to find a power animal. And when you have met your power animal, on yet another journey you might ask it what advice it has for you about a current opportunity or dilemma you are facing. It is best to have only one intention per journey.

If you are going to find a power animal, check your ego at the entrance. When you embark on this journey, be prepared to fully accept and embrace whatever the spirits offer. I remember well my first effort to retrieve an animal totem. I have always loved cats, and I was certain I was going down to get a nice big, powerful, sleek, awesome hunter. I was mired in my own ego. Imagine my shock when I saw a cow, then a close-up of a cow's eye, then a herd, and finally a little calf. I remember saying to myself, "You've got to be kidding me!" Well, the spirits always give you exactly what you need. Whether you like it or not, your power animal is always perfect for you. As for me, I had that masculine macho thing handled and didn't need a big cat. A cow is about nurturing. It is a provider of sustenance and clothing . . . a decidedly feminine energy. And that was perfect for me at that time. As fair warning on this issue, know three things:

1. I have never had anyone yet successfully predict what his or her power animal would be.
2. In addition to retrieving eagles, lions, and deer for others, I have also brought back ants, eels, squirrels, snakes, monkeys, and spiders.
3. It is not appropriate to reject a power animal and ask for another one. Trust that what you received is perfect for you. Just spend time with it and you will come to this realization yourself.

In order to learn about your power animal, its history, legend in myth, and meaning, I recommend a book titled *Animal-*

Speak: The Spiritual and Magical Powers of Creatures Great and Small by Ted Andrews (St. Paul: Llewellyn Publications, 1993). Mr. Andrews has written a second book titled *Animal-Wise: The Spirit Language and Signs of Nature* (Jackson, Tenn.: Dragonhawk Publishing, 1999), which contains background information on many animals not covered in his first book. A simpler and shorter animal book is *Medicine Cards: The Discovery of Power Through the Ways of Animals,* by Jamie Sams and David Carson (Santa Fe, N.M.: Bear & Company, 1988). You can also consult the web (www.animalspirits.com) for information about some animals.

The Journey

You are ready to start your journey now, but before you do, a couple of words of advice. First, the irony of a successful journey is that you let go of your need to control—you adopt the attitude of a curious child and release yourself into the entrance. But at the same time, you are in complete control, because anytime you want to end the journey, all you have to do is open your eyes. In a strange way you can have your cake and eat it too. You let go of your need to control and at the same time are in complete control.

Release any expectations you may have about what a journey may be like. Since each person's experience is different and you have not ever done a journey, how would you know what to expect in the first place? Too often people reject what they are legitimately experiencing because it doesn't fit their picture of what should be happening. The key is to trust that what is happening is exactly what is meant to occur that particular time.

Also, although it is not likely, if, during your journey, you see anything that you don't like, just go around it, retrace your steps back to your entrance, or simply open your eyes and remove your blindfold.

Nine Steps

1. **Lie down and relax.** The floor is probably better than your bed because you are less likely to fall asleep. Take at least three deep breaths, hold each at the end of your inhale for a few seconds, and then exhale until there is absolutely no breath left. Make each inhale-exhale cycle longer and deeper than the previous one.

2. **Put on your blindfold.** It will also help if the room is darkened.

3. **State your intention.** Do this in a relaxed manner. You are signaling to yourself and the spirit helpers what you want. Think of it as a respectful request rather than a goal to be pursued and achieved.

4. **Start the drumming.** Either start the tape or if you have a drummer, signal him or her to begin.

5. **Visualize your entrance to the earth and restate your intention several times.**

6. **Enter the entrance.** When you feel ready go into the entrance, you can go headfirst, feet first, or any way you like. Again, it doesn't matter if you have actually been in the entrance in your life or not. Also the entrance does not have to be bigger than you. For example, I have entered through a small opening in a tree that would never accommodate me in real life.

7. **Enjoy the journey.** Be prepared to experience the journey with any of your senses. For some it will be visual. Others will hear things. Others might smell or feel what is happening. Whatever sensory channel opens to you is the one to use for that particular journey. If you see something you don't like, go around it or

simply return by retracing your steps or opening your eyes, removing your blindfold. If you are journeying to find a power animal, look for an animal that shows itself to you four times. When that happens it is saying, "I am your power animal and am ready to return with you." It doesn't have to be the exact animal that shows itself four times. For example, when Mark found Wolf, he saw a real wolf but also saw a wolf emblazoned on a patch. If you are not certain, you can ask it if it is your power animal. But if you see it in four clear and different forms, you do not need any more proof. Trust that it is your power animal.

8. **Return from your journey.** It is a good idea to have a specified amount of time for each journey. Eight to ten minutes is what I usually recommend to begin with and up to fifteen minutes thereafter. Some drumming tapes are set to signal the "recall" for various times of duration. If someone is drumming for you, the recall is four sets of seven beats each (at a slightly slower interval than your journey drumming), followed by thirty seconds of very rapid drumming, followed by another four sets of seven beats. If you are journeying alone, you can set a watch alarm or a timer for the prescribed time. If you do this make sure the alarm is not so loud as to jar you out of your journey. When the recall sounds, it is time to return. To achieve this, simply do your journey in reverse. There is no need to rush, and it is not critical that you retrace your steps precisely. The reason for retracing your steps is to "groove" the journey so in subsequent trips you will be able to arrive and return from the lower world with greater ease and efficiency.

9. **Reflect on your journey.** When you have returned, relax for a moment. Don't try to get up right away. Notice how you feel. Reflect on what experiences you had and what you learned.

After the Journey

When the journey is complete, you might want to thank the spirits for supporting you in this effort and record it in a journal.

General Guidelines

1. Except for a power animal and, for more advanced journeying, a soul part, never bring anything back from the lower world with you.

2. Power animals and teachers (often in human form) will frequently communicate metaphorically. That is, they may behave in a certain way, and it is your job to interpret the behavior. For example, I recently journeyed for an audience before a speech, and my power animal first stretched his arms very wide and then did a little jig. To me that meant stretch or challenge them and play with them a bit. I did this and the feedback from the group was very good. It is your job and no one else's to get comfortable with this translating of behaviors. The first action of your power animal or teacher is always the most significant message. On some occasions your spirit helper might speak to you directly, particularly if you learn best through hearing.

3. Inevitably a newcomer will be in the middle of a journey and wonder, "Am I making this up?" The experience of those who journey regularly is that very rarely is this so. And since there is no way to answer that question, why not just decide that you are not creating it. If you say "Yes, I am making it up," you end the experience. If you say "No," you deepen it.

4. Be light and have fun with your journeying. It is an enjoyable experience, so have fun with it.

5. A journey is different from a dream. Dream interpretation is not what a journey is about.

6. Many people (not all) experience going through a tunnel at the beginning of a journey. If you feel yourself slowing down or not progressing, simply push on. If this doesn't work, you can return to your place of departure, restate your intention, and then start again. Sometimes it takes several journeys to negotiate the tunnel. Because everything is part of your journey, use being in the tunnel for extended time as a teaching. What is the message to you? What can you learn from it?

7. Be an observer during your journey, not a judge. Leave your critical mind when you start the journey and just enjoy the proceedings. And if you drift, gently bring yourself back to the voyage you have undertaken.

8. Allow the experience to unfold rather than rushing it or trying to force it. Michael Harner says that you are in charge of you while riding on a train, which is taking you to your chosen destination, but you are not in charge of the scenery or the inhabitants.

9. As strange as this may sound, take care of your power animal. It likes to visit our world as much as we enjoy a journey to its world. Study it, read about it, dance or move like it. Several times a week, invite it to join you in some activity. And most important, use it to empower you and give you advice. That is why it showed up, and you honor it when you allow it to achieve its purpose by helping you. You can journey to it and ask it what it needs from you for its well-being. If you choose not to use it, over time it will leave and, no doubt, seek someone who will use it well. This is simply a natural consequence of its not being honored or used.

10. Should you tell other people what your power animal is? Shamans differ on this. Some will never divulge their animals, while others will. The response I have gotten is that if it is in the service of healing work or with those close to me like my family, I can divulge my power animal(s). If it is frivolous (like at a cocktail party saying "I'm a lion, what are you?") it is inappropriate. The best thing to do is to journey to your power animal and find the answer directly.

11. Can you have more than one power animal? Yes. I have seven, and each is a specialist in a different aspect of shamanic work. The number of power animals you have has no relation to your effectiveness or ranking as a shamanic practitioner. In this case more has nothing to do with better.

The Shamanic Journey in Perspective

There are five conditions that will help you become a successful journeyer. They are:

1. **Let go of your need to control.** My experience is that this is difficult for most people to do in life, let alone in preparation for a meditative process like journeying. If you are trying to orchestrate your own journey you will be paying too much attention to the details and not be able to get into the flow required to really experience the lower world.

2. **Detach from outcomes.** This is also challenging for many of us. There is no way we can predict the outcome of a particular journey, yet so often we try. While we may have a mental image of what will happen, the experience never matches our picture. Release the image and enjoy the experience.

3. **Trust the spirit helpers.** A big help in letting go of your need to control and detaching from outcomes is to trust the spirit helpers. They will always orchestrate the perfect result for you. Whether you have an amazing experience in Technicolor, get held up in the tunnel, or don't experience any part of the journey at all, it is perfect for you at that time. As hard as it can be sometimes, trust that the spirits are giving you what you most need at that particular time.

4. **Lighten up and enjoy the experience.** My experience is that when you take all this too seriously, the spirit helpers will find a way to lighten things up. They are notorious tricksters and will always help you find the humor of your own seriousness.

5. **Leave your ego at the entrance.** As mentioned earlier in my cow story, when you think you are the center of the action, you are likely to miss the very important signals being given to you by the spirit helpers.

Let's see—let go of controls, detach from outcomes, trust, lighten up, and get out of your ego. This represents a life's journey for many of us. And what do you imagine would happen if we could create organizations that could engender these traits? Wouldn't going to work be much more pleasurable? The beauty of the process is that by learning how to journey and practicing what I have learned routinely I am continually training and conditioning myself to abandon my dysfunctional mind chatter and to approach life with both trust and lightness. The discipline of the shamanic journey has enabled me to be much more present in the company of another and a much more objective and capable observer of my own life. In and of itself, it has become a spiritual practice. I hope you will benefit as well.

Happy journeying!

Summary: The Nine Steps

1. Lie down and relax.
2. Blindfold on.
3. State intention.
4. Start drumming.
5. Visualize entrance and restate intention.
6. Enter the entrance.
7. Enjoy.
8. Return.
9. Reflect.

For More Information on Shamanism

1. Berggren, Karen A. *Circle of Shaman: Healing Through Ecstasy, Rhythm, and Myth*. Rochester, Vt.: Destiny Books, 1998.
2. Cowan, Tom. *Fire in the Head: Shamanism and the Celtic Spirit*. San Francisco: HarperSanFrancisco, 1993.
3. Cowan, Tom. *Shamanism as a Spiritual Practice for Daily Life*. Freedom, Calif.: Crossing Press, 1997.
4. Harner, Michael J. *The Way of the Shaman*. San Francisco: Harper & Row, 1990.
5. Ingerman, Sandra. *Medicine for the Earth: How to Transform Personal and Environmental Toxins*. New York: Three Rivers Press, 2000.
6. Ingerman, Sandra. *Soul Retrieval: Mending the Fragmented Self*. San Francisco: HarperSanFrancisco, 1991.
7. Ingerman, Sandra. *The Soul Retrieval Journey: Seeing in the Dark*. Audiocassette. Sounds True, 1997.
8. Ingerman, Sandra. *Welcome Home: Following Your Soul's Journey Home*. San Francisco: HarperSanFrancisco, 1993.
9. King, Serge Kahili. *Urban Shaman: A Handbook for Personal and Planetary Transformation Based on the Hawaiian Way of the Adventurer*. New York: Simon & Schuster, 1990.
10. Matthews, John. *The Celtic Shaman: A Handbook*. Boston: Element Books, 1991.

About the Author

Richard Whiteley is a successful entrepreneur and public speaker and a best-selling author. His first book, *The Customer Driven Company*, was named one of the top four business books of the year by *Fortune* magazine and one of the top ten books of the decade by *Human Resource Executive* magazine. In 1996, his *Customer Centered Growth* was named one of the top five business books by *Selling* magazine. His third book, *Love the Work You're With*, was published in 2001 and is a best-seller. For the past twenty-one years, Mr. Whiteley has engaged in a journey of personal growth during which he has studied with a number of acclaimed teachers in different parts of the world. In 1992 he was introduced to shamanism and began a training regimen in shamanic practice that continues today. He has presented this topic to the Young Presidents' Organization and other organizations. In addition to his writing and presentations, he has a small healing practice in Boston. Mr. Whiteley has a B.A. from Wesleyan University and an M.B.A. from Harvard Business School. He can be reached through his web site:
www.corpshaman.com

Mr. Whiteley can also be reached at:
richard@whiteleygroup.com
(617) 723-8889